*In The Path of Spiritual
goes well beyond what h*
describing for us the mos
*hidden parts of his journey in a riveting account of his
spiritual evolution. Unlike many writers who diminish
or skip entirely the role of Kundalini, jeff devotes a
lengthy chapter to Kundalini and its impact on his own
awakening. However, it is the chapter that follows that
is the real jewel in the lotus. In this penultimate section,
Jeff describes in magnificent detail his 'Journey Beyond
the Stars" in which he is indeed transported into mind
boggling mystical awareness. This is like a casket of jewels
left at your doorstep; a package of awakening pills you
are finally ready to consume; a bank account of spiritual
treasures with your name on it. Perhaps you have en-
countered a handful of similar accounts and you wonder
if there are even more. This is the journey into the heart
of mystery, the voyage into cosmic vastness beyond our
earthly sphere. Few are able to travel here and fewer
still able to speak of it with such eloquence and grace.
Your heart sings as you read. Each page bears the stamp
of authenticity. You immediately compile a mental list
of those you wish to share this brilliant writing with.
You immediately summon all your superlatives, all your
vocabulary of high praise. You include such descriptors
as stunning, amazing, astonishing, but then realize that
this experience is indeed ineffable, beyond the reach of
language, or thought. You are grateful to be brought this
close as witness of the eternal.*

- Dorothy Walters, Ph. D., Author of
*Kundalini Wonder: The god/goddess in Your Body;
The Goddess Speaks: Poems of Ecstasy and Transfiguration*

What a gift! Shoulder to shoulder, heart to heart, Jeff walks us through teachings and realizations that help us experience our own unique path of spiritual breakthrough. At the nexus of spiritual awakening and spiritual transformation stands this amazing offering.

~ Matt Ludmer, Founder of The Aligned Center

The Path of Spiritual Breakthrough , is perfect for anyone interested in what it looks and feels like inside the mind of a spiritual seeker. Jeff's wisdom, insight, vulnerability, and multi-dimensional perspective on spiritual awakening allows you to relax into your own evolutionary process. This book is a gift to anyone on the path.

~ Susan Kullman, Author of *Commit to What Is*

What if "spiritual breakthrough" was more about luminous allowance than heavy lifting? In this journey with Jeff one can receive pearls of cosmic reorientation, transmissions of embodied non-duality and golden reference points to the inner transformational compass. These are the necessary ingredients for a true Metamorphosis. And indeed these are times of metamorphosis. The Path of Spiritual Breakthrough is not just a story of spiritual heroism, it's an ally for souls who long to be embodiments of freedom and naturalness in this life. It is rare to read spiritual text that can be digested and integrated with such ease and deliciousness. And this is perhaps what I love most about this journey with Jeff.

~ Tiffany Carole, cultural midwife

Jeff has the rare and beautiful gift of being able to take deep spiritual and philosophical concepts and share them in a personal and accessible way. The Path of Spiritual Breakthrough feels like a behind-the-scenes tour into the unknown, given by a trusted friend and teacher. As with all of Jeff's work, this book is an invitation to explore the generous possibilities waiting for you in your life.

– Erin Aquin, Master Certified Life Coach,
Author of *Revitalize Your Relationship*

I love this book. When Jeff writes, you feel the undercurrent of an energy that touches your heart. He writes as though he is writing to the inner dimensions of your being. Each word, each sentence, is a carrier of vibrancy. In The Path Of Spiritual Breakthrough, I was deeply struck by Jeff's vulnerability and profound courage in sharing his innermost teachings and spiritual experiences. I left this book viscerally excited to explore the unplumbed depths of my own spiritual journey.

– Louis Parsons, SoulScape Artist

An articulate and captivating description of the path toward spiritual understanding.

– Ralph Strauch, Ph.D. Author of
The Reality Illusion, How you make the world you experience

Other Books in this Series:
The Mystical Philosophy of Jeff Carreira

The Soul of a New Self: Embracing the Future of Being Human
by Jeff Carreira.

Paradigm Shifting: Guiding Evolution from the Inside
by Jeff Carreira.

Higher Self Expression: How to Become an Artist of Possibility
by Jeff Carreira.

Free Resources from Jeff Carreira

Life Without Fear: Meditation as an Antidote to Anxiety
with Jeff Carreira. Visit lifewithoutfear.online

Secrets of Profound Meditation: Six Spiritual Insights that will Transform Your Life with Jeff Carreira.
Visit secretsofprofoundmeditation.com

Foundations of a New Paradigm: A 6-part program designed to shift the way you experience everything with Jeff Carreira.
Visit foundationsofanewparadigm.com

THE PATH OF SPIRITUAL BREAKTHROUGH

FROM AWAKENING TO COSMIC AWARENESS

ISBN: 978-1-954642-12-6

Emergence Education
P.O. Box 63767
Philadelphia, PA 19147
EmergenceEducation.com

Cover design by Olivia Wu.
Original cover art by Jeff Carreira.

Printed in the United States of America.

THE PATH OF SPIRITUAL BREAKTHROUGH

FROM AWAKENING TO COSMIC AWARENESS

JEFF CARREIRA

EMERGENCE EDUCATION

Philadelphia, Pennsylvania

Contents

Introduction

THIS BOOK OFFERS DETAILS OF a journey of spiritual awakening and transformation, but more importantly it is a phenomenological exploration of that journey, meaning that it focuses on the *experience* of awakening and the *experience* of transformation. We will explore the significance of extraordinary breakthrough experiences and speculate as to what they might have to tell us about who we are and how reality works.

It will be a fascinating exploration, taking us to some of the furthest edges of the possible. Some of our most basic assumptions about what it means to be human will be called into question. There will be times when you may look at yourself and not know who you are anymore. This is not just a book about transformation, it is a transformative journey. Engaging with the ideas and perspectives that are presented in these pages can shift your perception of everything.

For this reason, I ask you to read this book with one eye on the words and the other on your own internal responses to the word. Words can have a profound and magical effect on our state of consciousness. Certain ideas, presented clearly to an open mind, can shift our experience. You will find in these pages, ideas that have the power to shift your consciousness. For that reason I suggest that as you read, you pay attention to any shifts that you experience and always remain open to having more.

CHAPTER ONE

Spiritual Awakening

*"I remembered how, a little child, I had stopped myself
one day on the stairs, and asked, how came I here? How
is it that I seem to be this Margaret Fuller? What does
it mean? What shall I do about it? I remembered all the
times and ways in which the same thought had returned.
I saw how long it must be before the soul can learn to act
under these limitations of time and space, and human
nature; but I saw, also, that it Must do it, — that it
must make all this false true, — and sow new and
immortal plants in the garden of God; before it could
return again. I saw there was no self; that selfishness was
all folly, and the result of circumstance; that it was only
because I thought self real that I suffered; that I had
only to live in the idea of the All, and all was mine. This
truth came to me, and I received it unhesitatingly; so
that I was for that hour taken up into God."*

- Margaret Fuller

IN THIS BOOK WE'LL BE using lots of words and phrases that you're undoubtedly familiar with, yet the meaning of them often remains elusive. "Spiritual Awakening" is one such phrase. What does it mean for someone to be spiritually awake? Are we ourselves one of those people who is awake?

I define spiritual awakening as the realization that there is more to reality than the sum total of everything we've ever known or have been told exists. One way that we could describe this is to say that we have woken up to the mystery of the unknown unknown.

We could say that reality consists of the known, the unknown and the unknown unknown. The known is simply everything that we know. I know I am a man. I know I live in Philadelphia. I know that Portugal is a country on the Iberian Peninsula. I know what Lisbon airport looks like because I've been there. We all know so much, but we don't know everything, and we know that we don't know everything.

The unknowns are all the things that we know that we don't know. I don't know the population of Cincinnati. I don't know the driving distance between Paris and Madrid. I don't know the scientific names of the plants in my backyard. I don't know any of these things and so much more. But I know that I don't know them, and I know that it would be possible to learn them if I needed to.

The last category is the unknown unknown. This is the mysterious category of things that I don't have the slightest inkling even exist. These are things that I usually assume are impossible until they aren't. They are the impossible possibilities. When we discover something that we didn't even know could have existed, we open to the realm of the unknown unknown. The discovery of the unknown unknown is what wakes us up spiritually. What does it wake us up to? Infinite possibility. When we discover that existence includes unknown unknowns we come into direct contact with the infinite. Why? Because suddenly we don't know what the limits of reality are. For some of us, the discovery of the unknown unknown diminishes our interest in anything else.

Once you discover that things you thought could not exist might be possible, nothing is ever the same. You enter into an experience of unlimited possibility. I remember one particularly vivid moment of this realization in my own spiritual history. It happened when I was on a meditation retreat. I had been on retreat for at least three weeks at that point. There were only twelve people participating in the retreat. We were waking up at 4:00am and doing spiritual practice, mainly meditation, until 10:00pm.

I had already been experiencing miraculous things everyday during the first three weeks of the retreat. I had seen so many impossible possibilities that I was losing my bearings. We stay anchored in our current sense of reality largely by referencing what we think is, and is not, possible. The dividing line that separates the possible from the impossible creates the border of our reality. Having a good solid border defining reality is a very positive thing. If you didn't know what was possible and what was impossible it would be very difficult to live. Imagine that with each step you couldn't be completely certain that the ground would hold your weight. How would you muster the courage to walk if you might fall through to the center of the earth at any moment.

Normally, having a solid sense of what is and what is not possible is very important for our sanity. That is why deep spiritual work is not necessarily a good idea for every person at every time in their life, or for every temperament. In traditional spiritual work there were safeguards against harm. If you were a Buddhist monk in Tibet, or a Christian nun in the middle ages, you would work for years preparing for the higher esoteric teachings that were designed to open you beyond the possible. By the time a monk came to the point when the esoteric teachings would be offered, they would have proven themselves to be stable and dedicated enough to do the higher work.

Today, the situation is different. Some of the highest esoteric mystical philosophies and practices are available online at the click of a button with no preparation required at all. You can receive these teachings and practices without the benefit of an experienced guide or teacher and completely outside any institutional structure designed to support your journey.

Of course, there was never any guarantee that the safeguards put in place in traditional religious settings would work either. Plenty of things went wrong, and continue to go wrong, within traditions. It is also true that the demands of modern life, pursuing formal education, holding a job, and simply navigating through the complexities of living, in many ways can be seen as preparation for intensive spiritual work. The bottom line is, in the modern spiritual marketplace we each have to take responsibility for our own choices. We must be careful who we choose to trust, and which practices we engage with. Today we are faced with a vast array of choices from which to create a spiritual path and it is one of my hopes for this book that what you discover by reading it will help you make informed spiritual choices in the future. It also must be said that although deep spiritual work can be done intelligently, I don't know that it can be done risk free.

In the interest of full disclosure, I would now like to divulge a little more about myself. A great deal of my most intensive spiritual training took place over a twenty year period in which I lived in a radical spiritual practice community. Many people who were part of that community would insist that it was a cult, and I cannot entirely disagree. It was a world unto itself. We had a charismatic leader to whom we gave excessive authority and too much benefit of the doubt. We subjected ourselves to what were at times grueling, harsh and arguably abusive circumstances.

That being said, I also experienced profoundly life-altering realizations regularly, sometimes on a daily basis. For me the growth potential was enormous and I can honestly say that the person I am now, the one who left that community after twenty years, is a dramatically transformed version of the person who entered. When I think back to the person I was before that time, I can see that it was me who entered the community, but the person I was then could never imagine the person I am today. And most importantly the growth that I experienced was overwhelmingly positive in spite of the many flaws in the system that I was a part of. This was not everyone's experience. Many people would tell you that they are worse off for their time there. My heart goes out to them, and I hope that they have found healing and resolution.

What you will find in this book is an exploration largely based on the experiences of revelation that I had during those twenty years and in the nearly ten years since. You will see as you read on, that I learned, or at least hope I learned, as much from the things that went wrong as I did from the miracles that occurred. One of the things that I left with was a strong sense that deep spiritual work comes with no guarantees. There is a risk no matter what you do. Of course, that applies to all of life. Life is not guaranteed either. In fact that was the first truly life-altering spiritual realization I had on the path.

It happened the first time I went to see a talk given by the teacher whose community I would later join. By that time I had been on the spiritual path in my own willy nilly way for about a decade. I can't say I remember a specific moment when I awakened to the reality of the unknown unknown. Instead, from a very young age, I had always had a sense that nothing that I was being told about myself, the world around me, or the meaning of human life, made complete sense. It all seemed so small. I had friends and I enjoyed the company of other people, but I always felt alone in the world because I knew what everyone seemed to accept as the limits of what was possible, was not. It would be many more years before I would realize why I felt that way at such a young age.

The first time I remember engaging in something that you could call spiritual practice, was at about the age of seven. I would sit in my father's car and try to make my thoughts stop. When that proved impossible, I tried looking for a crack between thoughts that I could escape through. When that didn't work either, I surrendered to what appeared to be my fate, imprisonment within the confines of my mind. A few years later I started my next spiritual practice. This time it was laying on the grass on beautiful summer nights looking up at the stars. I could do the same thing on lazy afternoons looking up at the clouds floating overhead. In either case I would quickly be overcome by a sense of the enormous size of the planet I had found myself on and its minuscule size compared to the rest of the universe. As I would contemplate the size of an infinite universe, I would feel electrical impulses of recognition shooting up and down my spine, an energy that today, I would call the arising of Kundalini, but of course as a child I had no idea about such things. Those hours of quiet contemplation were some of the most pleasurable of my life.

Some people distinctly remember waking up. In my case I distinctly remember deciding to go back to sleep. By the time I was in the fifth grade, I was not an entirely happy boy. I found it difficult to be at ease around other people. I was shy and awkward and anxious most of the time. Then one night something happened. I was watching a sitcom on television. One of the characters in the show was a guy who was always joking around in a slightly annoying, but ultimately endearing way. Everyone loved that person and he seemed to be free and easy with himself and everyone around him. As I watched the show, I suddenly realized that I could be that person. I could be the funny guy that was always joking around and that everyone loved to be with. So the very next day at school I went as that guy and not as myself. I was cracking jokes, mostly bad, all day long. My few friends told me to stop. They said I was making a fool of myself, but I just kept going. No one liked me or my jokes for weeks, but slowly I started to become more funny. I was talking to more people. I started to fit in.

Two years later my semi-conscious assimilation project completed itself. I was now in seventh grade and I had to give a speech in my English class. It was an election year and we were asked to pretend to be a candidate. I was terrified. Public speaking was my absolute biggest fear. The idea of standing in front of a classroom full of my peers and speaking was my worst nightmare. I remember sitting at my desk, knowing that it was my turn next and being almost paralyzed with fear. When the person before me finished the teacher called my name. I stood up.

At that moment I made a decision. I was not going to give this speech as myself because I couldn't. I was going to become someone else. I was going to be a political candidate and give the speech as that person. I stood up and looked out at my classmates, but it wasn't me. I was playing a role now. I was a candidate giving a speech, and I gave a truly rousing speech. I remember finishing having no real memory of what had just happened. I looked around and I could see the surprise on all of my classmates' faces. The teacher applauded. "That was fantastic Jeff," he said. "You should go into politics."

That day I discovered that the way you fit into this world is by playing a role. All you have to do is choose who you want to be and then just be that person. I had made it. I was on the inside now. I didn't feel alienated anymore. I felt normal. But, without realizing it I had managed to forget who I truly was and fall back asleep, I stopped worrying about bigger things. I stopped being fascinated by what existed beyond my mind. The problem was, my assimilation didn't stick very well. For a few years, right through high school I managed to fit in by staying in character, but there was always a part of me that knew the person that I had become was not me. I knew I was playing a role and I wasn't completely comfortable knowing that.

Before going further, I first want to go back to that first night when I met the person who would for a long time become my spiritual teacher. I had been reading the book he had written and I had resonated deeply with everything in it, but I had one burning question and I asked it as soon as I mustered the courage. Sitting in front of him I asked, "Everything in your book seems more true to me than anything else I know, but how do I find the faith to give myself to it, and know that everything will turn out OK?"

He looked back at me with what I later realized was a characteristic intensity. He said almost tauntingly, "Who says everything is going to be OK? This could all turn out to be a big mess. If you knew everything was going to turn out OK, you wouldn't need any faith would you? There are no guarantees in this life. The part of you that wants a guarantee, is the part that's getting its head dragged to the chopping block. What I'm offering is a one way ticket. You get on this train and you never come back."

He went on talking for another 10 minutes, but honestly, I don't remember anything else that he said that day. I knew he was right, and knowing that put me at a crossroads. I now had to choose, would I follow this path or would I go back to the life I had been living just a few hours before? Suddenly, my mind was blown. The room swirled and got dizzy. I seemed to have a life review experience and I saw that I had always tried to play it safe. I was always trying to figure out what actions would lead to the best outcome. What I had just learned was that even playing it safe carries risk. There was no way for me to avoid the implications of what I had just realized.

In a journal at the time, which later became one of my first books, I wrote these words to express what I learned that day.

> Human life is a risk.
> To believe in anything is a risk.
> To not believe is also a risk.
>
> Anything we do is a risk.
> Not doing anything is a risk.
>
> We might decide to avoid risk by believing nothing
> and doing nothing.
> That's risky.
>
> Better to believe wholeheartedly,
> always ready to think again
> and change our minds.

I was faced with what the great American philosopher and psychologist, William James described as a "momentous and forced choice". I had to choose how to live. I had to choose to dedicate myself entirely to a spiritual life, or not. This choice was forced because I could not avoid it. I now saw clearly that giving all of my energy and attention to the pursuit of spiritual liberation and illumination was a real possibility, where choosing to do it, or not, were my only options Once one sees the possibility of living a spiritual life, it becomes a forced choice that cannot be avoided. That is why some spiritual traditions warn not to start on the path if you don't intend to go all the way to the finish.

Before we awaken to the unknown unknown, we simply accept that the boundaries and parameters that we have been taught are real and cannot be surmounted. We may not like the limitations, we may want to live beyond them, but we cannot even imagine how. And remember, we are not talking about boundaries that lie within existence and separate this part from that part. We are talking about the boundary at the edge of existence itself. The edge of the possible. One of the things that we will do in this book is challenge the boundaries of existence. We will walk together to the edge and look beyond it into the impossible and the unknowable. Once you get a glimpse that impossible possibilities do in fact exist, you can't go back. You can choose to ignore them, but that will be just as much a choice as choosing to follow them.

My recognition of the inherent risk of life had catapulted me beyond the point of no return. There was no way back. I couldn't unsee what I had seen and now I had to decide how I was going to respond. There was no way to avoid responding, because to not respond was itself a response. I realized that there was no way to not make a choice. I was experiencing a kind of total responsibility for my own life.

Here I want to expand on my original definition of awakening. Spiritual awakening is more than just seeing greater possibilities, it also means recognizing that we are alive and in the middle of an actual life. We habitually live our lives as if they haven't started yet. We are culturally conditioned to spend a great deal of our time and energy in preparation for the future. It is as if we are preparing and rehearsing for a life that will soon begin. Part of spiritual awakening is waking up to the fact that life has already started and you are already in the middle of it. Life is like a playing field that has no sidelines. The game has started, and there's nowhere off the field to warm up, practice, or rehearse. No matter where you go, you are still in the game, and no matter what you do, it is all part of the game. There is no way out. Every choice you make counts, and every time you delay choosing that is also a choice that counts.

The realization of this depth of immediacy can be overwhelming. Suddenly we feel like we don't have any room to maneuver. Everything we do counts, every moment has consequences, there is no place to stand that won't have an effect. On the one hand this feels overwhelming. On the other hand, it feels thrilling. It is the feeling of recognizing that you are alive. You are here. This is it! After that night, when I saw the inherent risk of life, I felt the immediacy of the fact that I had to decide what kind of life I was going to live. I could delay the decision, but delaying was a decision too, with its own consequences.

It was so thrilling because I saw how my life had always been built moment by moment according to the choices I made, even if the choice was to wait and choose later. I hadn't known that my hesitation and delays were having an effect. I was living as if delaying a decision had no consequence and I had all the time in the world to decide. Now I knew that everything was always having an effect all of the time. Now I saw how to live a more conscious life by actively making choices, even if the choice was to delay making a decision. All of those choices could be made consciously, knowing that they all had consequences. I finally understood what it meant to be conscious. I was thrilled and I knew that I was going to drop everything in my life and devote myself entirely to spiritual work, so I could live the most deeply conscious life possible.

You can be awake in the sense that you realize there is more to reality than the sum total of everything you've ever known or been told about, without experiencing the immediate implications of that. For example, some people see the vastness of reality in a flash of insight, but don't feel compelled to do anything about it. Something triggered a spiritual awakening, but the implications of that awakening did not seem to be revealed, or if they were revealed, they were ignored. In these cases the awakening experience gradually fades away. It becomes a vague memory of something that happened, and eventually it is forgotten all together.

This happened in a dramatic way to someone I know. I had already been living in a spiritual community for a number of years when an old friend called me. He told me that the night before he had been out at a bar having drinks with his best friend and his best friend's father. They had a fun time laughing and joking over a few beers. The next morning his best friend called him distraught. It seemed that his father had died overnight in his sleep. Sharing beers together in the bar was his last act.

When my friend called he was also distraught, not from grief so much as revelation. "We will all go that way. One minute we will be here having a beer, then we will just be gone. Where do we go? My friend's dad was so alive just last night. Where is he now?" In his distress my friend was expressing both halves of the spiritual awakening experience. His contemplation about where we go after death shows that he was awake to the mystery beyond the known, and his realization that we will all die at some random moment had brought him in touch with the immediate preciousness of existence.

As he continued to speak, the full breadth of the revelation revealed itself. "We live like we are going to be here forever." He said. "We just go to work and earn money and go out for beers, and we always assume that there will be a tomorrow, but one day there isn't. One day we're gone. When we really know that we aren't going to be here forever we can't just go on living in the same way. What's the point in working, earning money, and having fun, if we just disappear one day. It doesn't make sense. I don't understand."

That night my friend and I spoke on the phone for a few hours. He had never been interested in my spiritual life, but suddenly he wanted to know all about it - and everything I told him made perfect sense. Now he understood why I had left everything to join a spiritual community. We had been friends since childhood, but we had never had any profound conversations about spirituality. It was all different now. We were in the same world. We talked about the mysteries of being and the delicate and wonderful potential of being alive. To me he seemed to be utterly reborn. He was fully alive and lit up by a profound spiritual view of human life.

About a week later we talked again, but something was different. Our conversation had reverted back to what it had been before his awakening. We spoke about news of the world, mutual friends, and non-spiritual interests. After a while I asked him what had happened. I wanted to know if he was still thinking about the mysterious precariousness of life on Earth. He said, as if remembering, "Oh that... it went away. I'm kind of glad. I had found it hard to function while I kept thinking about all that stuff."

We spoke a while longer and it was clear that whatever had happened the week before was gone. I prodded a few times, but there was nothing there. He remembered the things he had said, but they weren't alive for him anymore. They were just memories. They didn't matter, in fact, he was glad that they had died.

In order for an experience of spiritual awakening to have power it must be alive. It must matter to us. It can't be something that we can just ignore. It has to present us with an unavoidable decision point - a point of no return.

For me, what created that intensity was the recognition that life was inherently risky and there was no way to live that was guaranteed to work out. Seeing that every life contained risk, meant that the life that I was living, the one in which I was trying to figure out what was the right thing to do, was just as risky as any other. As I already said, when I had that realization, I experienced a life-review. I saw my life of seeking security, I saw it continuing and I realized that in the end it would not be meaningful. I knew I could not continue as I was. I needed to shift into a new life. But I also knew that any life I chose would be equally risky.

The author, Carlos Castaneda, wrote numerous books in the 1960's and 70's that captured the spiritual imaginations of millions of people. I came across those books decades after they had first appeared, but still, they captivated me. I became entranced by Castaneda's account of his alleged apprenticeship with the Yaqui sorcerer known as Don Juan Matus.

One of the things that Castaneda learned from Matus was that death should always be your guide in life. In one of his books there is a description of how death appears as a car driving behind Castaneda on a highway at night. The headlights of the car are always catching up with him. Matus laughed and explained that it was not a car gaining on them from behind, it was death. Death is always behind us, Matus explained, but we don't always see it because sometimes it doesn't have its headlights on.

The death of my friend's acquaintance had turned the headlights of death on in his rear-view mirror. He expressed clearly during that first conversation that death was always behind us and might catch up with us at any time. The same thing happened to me when I realized the inherent risk in life. I was very aware that my life was going to end and that if I kept on seeking for security I would die seeking for security. I saw clearly now that no life was inherently any more secure than any other. They were all a risk. In fact, with death as my guide, I saw that any life choice was a 50/50 gamble - it was either going to work out or it wasn't.

In the wake of my realization of the inherent risk of life I contemplated the inevitability of the end of my life. I imagined myself at some as yet undisclosed time in the future knowing that I only had a few hours until my time in this body would come to an end. I've heard it said that during those last hours of life you gain a radical clarity on things. There is no longer any reason to lie to yourself and so you find yourself being honest and transparent. I really tried to imagine what it might be like to have literally no time left. What would be important to me then? As I thought about this I realized that what would be important to me would be that I gave everything in life. What would leave me full of regrets in those last hours would be realizing that I had compromised on what I truly cared about. I wouldn't want to come to that moment of passing and realize that I hadn't even tried to live the life I really wanted.

Everything changed in my life after that experience . Within a year I had amicably left what, by any normal standard, had been a good marriage as well as my job as an engineer and I moved into a spiritual community. Nothing was ever going to be the same. In comparison, after having a similar existential realization about the inevitability of death, my friend's life didn't change at all. It was disrupted for a week or two, but then he slotted back into his old grooves.

Why is it that similar, and sometimes identical spiritual experiences can end up having such dramatically different results? Why does one person's life change irrevocably, and another's not at all? These are the kinds of questions we will explore in this book. And given that I don't like to hold back the finale, I will tell you the short answer now.

The reason why similar or even identical spiritual experiences can result in dramatically different types and degrees of change is because of how each individual interprets and makes meaning out of the experience or experiences they have. As we will explore in this book, this is a much more profound matter than it might at first seem. In order to understand the full significance of this we will need to challenge our most fundamental understanding of reality itself.

Jeff Carreira

CHAPTER TWO

Creative Illumination

"In art and dream proceed with abandon."

- Patti Smith

BEFORE WE GO ANY FURTHER I want to share some thoughts about the nature of reality, because unless we do, it will be hard to get very far in our exploration. I'm going to start this chapter with one of my favorite quotations. It comes from the philosopher Alfred North Whitehead, who states:

It takes a very unusual mind to undertake the analysis of the obvious.

Ontology is the branch of philosophy that asks the question "What is real?" This is a profoundly difficult question to ask. The reason it's so difficult to ask, is because the way we answer most questions is by comparing them to something that we know is real. If I ask if a house is white, I just need to look at the color of it and compare it to what I already know white is. I can answer the question either yes or no, but only if I already know what the color white really looks like. If I don't already know what white is, how can I possibly answer the question?

We can only determine the truth of something by comparing it to something we already know is true. With this kind of questioning we can question anything, but we can't question everything at the same time. There has to be something that we already know is true so that we can determine the validity of whatever it is that we are asking about. When we ask "What is real?" we lose our footing, because we are questioning the basis of all knowing.

We need to unpack this a little so that we can understand the dilemma that we are going to face in the rest of this book. We think of ourselves as living in reality, but it is probably more accurate that we live inside a definition of reality, a paradigm - a set of assumptions about what is real that everything else is forced to conform to. We have an idea about what reality is, but how do we know if we are right? We all emerge into life inside a culture, and that culture holds certain ideas about what is real. Anything that aligns with those ideas appears to us as real. Anything that appears to be in conflict with those ideas is assumed to be unreal. This is crucial to our exploration, because our mystical and spiritual experiences often veer beyond what is believed to be real, into the unreal - by both other people and ourselves.

Even more profoundly, experiences that we have that lie beyond the limits of our set of assumed beliefs about reality are often unconsciously filtered out of our conscious experience. That means we might experience phenomena outside of our current reality all the time, without ever realizing. It is my belief that there are many people who have had profound spiritual and mystical experiences, and don't even realize it. These experiences are simply removed from view before they become aware of them.

There is a wonderful Awareness Test video that you can find on YouTube that illustrates this point beautifully. (Spoiler alert if you read the rest of this paragraph the video will not work for you, so if you want to experience it for yourself I suggest you find it and try it before you read on.) In the video there are two teams of people each with one basketball between them. One team is wearing white, the other black. The video asks you to count how many times the white team passes the ball back and forth. Both teams start moving. All the players begin weaving in and out between each other while passing their basketball to their teammates. At the end, the video tells you that the white team passed the ball 13 times. But then it asks you if you noticed the dancing bear that went by. If you are like me, at that point you are sure there was no dancing bear in the video. The tape is rolled backwards and sure enough as the players of both teams are weaving in and out and passing the balls a large black bear dances slowly across the screen between them all. At that point I was certain that the bear had not been there the first time I watched and must have been spliced in later so I played the video again. The bear was there from the start. I was amazed.

So what is happening here? You have been asked to count how many times the white team passes the ball. To keep count, you have to pay careful attention to all of the players dressed in white, and ignore all of the players dressed in black as they weave in and out between each other. Since the bear is also black, your eyes ignore the bear too. The end result is that you don't notice the bear in the video at all. The instructions basically tell you that only the players in white matter. They are the ones that are real to you and so they are the ones you watch for. You follow them so closely that you miss an obvious dancing bear in the middle of the scene. I am sure the metaphor here is clear. The instructions represent the assumptions of the paradigm we live in, they tell us what is real and therefore what to pay attention to. Things that do not match up with our current beliefs about reality are filtered out of conscious experience. We simply don't see the dancing bear.

When I say that we don't live in reality, because we live in a paradigm, what I mean is that how we see the world is shaped by a set of assumptions and instructions that tell us what is important to pay attention to and what is not. Those guidelines live inside us and they create the experience of reality we have. What our spiritual experiences reveal to us is that there is much more possible than we have been taught. When we experience things that break the rules of what is supposed to be possible, our experience of reality expands. And it only takes one reality expanding experience to change everything, because now you know anything is possible. A spiritual experience doesn't prove that everything is possible, but it does show you that you don't know what's possible and because you don't know, then effectively anything is. This book is about two things. First, just how much bigger and more bizarre reality might be than we think. And second, that we might just have much more control over our experience of reality than we think.

The Western world is largely living in a paradigm that was established during the age of Enlightenment and rests on two fundamental assumptions. The first is that there is only one reality. If two people see things differently, then it stands to reason that one of them, or maybe both, must be wrong. Reality is an either/ or event. Reality can only be one way. So, the first assumption that we live under is that there is only one reality. It must also be said that more recently Western culture has embraced relativism, meaning that we can accept more than one point of view as real, but ultimately only relatively real. Culturally, this embrace of relativism has done a great service to humanity because it allows for previously marginalized perspectives to be accepted and honored. Still, even in relativism, there is a belief that underneath all of the various perspectives and points of view there is one real reality.

In our current paradigm there is no robust way to imagine that two people could hold two different views about what is real, that are both absolutely not just relatively true. Those of us who feel compelled to follow the path of spiritual revelation into higher dimensions of reality will need to find a way to do this. We must begin to embrace a view of reality that allows more than one thing to be true at the same time. We must move from a universe to a multiverse. If there is one reality, then we live in a paradigm of exclusivity in which there can only be one truth and all other possibilities must be false. If we have a spiritual experience which reveals something that should not be possible, our cultural tendency will be to dismiss it as unreal. That experience, along with the possibility that it hinted at, will most likely be banished from your mind before you even become conscious of it, and therefore it will never be embraced. Before we can voyage to higher dimensions of reality, we must learn to accept ontological multiplicity by embracing the paradox of more than one truth.

If you think about it for a minute you will find that it is difficult to even imagine two things being both contradictory and true. For example, a person has to be either 16 years old or not 16 years old. She can't be both 16 and 39 years old. If you spend a minute thinking about this you will see that your mind cannot relate to the idea of someone being both 16 and 39 years old at the same time. We are not allowed to accept two different versions of truth that are simultaneously contradictory and true. But this kind of multiplicity of truth is exactly what I am saying we need to be able to embrace if we want to open to the strange new worlds that our spiritual experiences invite us into. If we can't open to the paradox of multiple realities, then our spiritual experiences will almost always be filtered out of mind before we become conscious of them. And even if one manages to float up into conscious awareness, you will immediately feel compelled to prove that it is either real or unreal, and the current paradigm will be overwhelmingly biased toward convincing you to dismiss it, which is probably what you will end up doing. In fact, you have probably already done this without realizing it many times. There is no way for us to know how many spiritual realizations have been filtered out of our experience before we were even aware of them, and we probably don't remember all the times we offhandedly dismissed a bizarre experience that might have been a mystical opening.

One way to hold the paradox of multiplicity is to imagine

that reality is not fixed and static. Instead, imagine that reality is in constant flux, always shifting and morphing under our feet. The reality of this moment is not the reality of the moment before or the moment after. Don't imagine each moment as a new moment in the same reality. Imagine each moment arising as a complete reality. That means that the experience of the past and the experience of the future are arising right now in the present moment. What if a minute ago you were a child in India. As that child, you had a memory of the life you had lived up until that moment, and a set of aspirations for a future that you imagined for yourself. Then in the next moment, you were whoever you are now, with memories of your current past, and dreams of a different future. The next moment brings an entirely new life. Then another. Of course, there is no reason to believe this is the case, but if you think about it, there is no way to prove for certain that it isn't either. The more you explore wild and bizarre possibilities, the more you realize that reality might be more strange than you can even imagine.

Yes, I know, this sounds too bizarre to even think about, but here's the thing, many of our spiritual experiences are too bizarre to think about too. That part of us that dismisses the bizarre is exactly the part of us we need to override. Reality is much more bizarre than we think. Spiritual experiences open us to some unthinkably bizarre aspects of reality. If we want these experiences to catapult us into a new reality, we must be ready to embrace the truly strange.

I have had the opportunity to speak about these things with two brilliant scholars, Timothy Morton and Jeffrey J. Kripal, both currently at Rice University. In a phone conversation with Timothy Morton he described how our culture contains antibodies to weirdness. These cultural antibodies seek out and destroy any weird experiences or ideas we might hold. In our bodies, antibodies protect us from illness. In a culture the weirdness antibodies protect us from breeches in our beliefs about reality. The paradigm we live in is a set of assumptions about reality. As long as the paradigm is not fundamentally challenged, life goes on smoothly. But if the paradigm is called into question in any significant way, the entire edifice could fall apart, leaving us lost in the uncertainty of the unknown unknown. The dominant paradigm in a culture will protect itself against fundamental uncertainty. We will experience that defense in ourselves as our own dismissive attitude toward the unusual and the bizarre. Those of us who are pursuing dramatic spiritual revelation and transformation must find a way to override this cultural defense mechanism.

The second conversation I want to mention was with Jeffrey J. Kripal. Jeffrey is a professor of religious studies and has become a good friend over the past few years. During one of our many conversations, I described to him two of my earliest childhood spiritual experiences. After I had explained them, he commented on something I had missed. He noted that in both cases I described having locked myself safely behind closed doors before allowing the experience to occur. In one instance I had locked myself in my parents bathroom, in the other I was locked in my father's car. He noted that even at a young age I knew that it was not safe to have these experiences in public and needed to keep them a secret. Those of us who have had powerful spiritual openings often find that they do not receive a warm reception if we share about them with others. These stories are often met with disinterest, disbelief, and sometimes hostility. When someone is open to hearing about these experiences it is generally because they have had one of their own.

The cultural antibodies against weirdness exist in us and in the people around us. These antibodies exist as prejudiced attitudes and beliefs that very effectively ward off the possibility of anything unexpected ever happening. On those rare occurrences where something bizarre actually arises into consciousness, the antibodies will almost always ensure that we dismiss it before any damage can be done to our current belief system. I am writing this book to help you open beyond these cultural defense systems. I am assuming that you are someone who wants to experience the ultimate, who is not afraid to have their understanding of reality fundamentally questioned, and probably already has good reason to believe that reality is very different than any of us assumes.

I believe that an important step that many of us need to take before we can liberate our awareness from the confines of the current paradigm is to question the assumptions of our materialistic paradigm. We don't have to dismiss materialism or totally embrace some other point of view, but we do need to be willing to seriously question it and open to the possibility of a very different reality.

In a materialistic paradigm, reality is assumed to be primarily a physical space filled with material objects. That is the paradigm we live in. We assume that reality is a universe of three dimensions of empty space filled with interacting but separate things. As long as this is our foundational belief about what reality is, there is very little room for us to accept the reality of our spiritual experiences. If the foundational belief we hold about reality is unquestionable then any experience we have will be forced to conform to it. Any experience we have that cannot be made to fit into our foundational beliefs will be explained away.

On meditation retreats I have experienced myself as a cosmic being, literally as one with the compassionate wisdom at the core of the universe. I am certain that in these instances I am inhabiting a very real aspect of who I am. At some level, I am a cosmic being. But I have spoken to many people who either think that I'm delusional or that the hours of practice somehow altered my brain chemistry so that I had such a strange experience. The idea that someone can be delusional, or can have strange experiences due to altered brain chemistry, are two ways of taking an inexplicable experience and making it conform to the limitations of the current paradigm. These people are initially troubled by what I tell them because it is calling their bottom line beliefs into question. But once they come up with an explanation that works within the paradigm of scientific materialism that we have all been enculturated into, they can relax.

William James was a pioneering American psychologist. He was one of the most prominent academic intellectuals of his time and he did not believe in a universe of three dimensional space filled with things. James believed in a reality that was created out of pure experience. He was a proponent of idealism rather than materialism. A materialist believes that reality is fundamentally a physical space filled with material stuff. An idealist believes that reality is fundamentally created from mental stuff, more like a dream. In this book I am going to ask you to consider this possibility. I don't mean for you to embrace that worldview as your own, just to consider it as a way to open your sense of possibility.

For an idealist, first there was some kind of mind, an absolute intelligence or pure consciousness. In many religious traditions this initiating source of existence is called God. From this mind the world, the universe and all forms of living beings are born. Mind was here first and then matter formed out of mind. Idealism stands in contrast to materialism, which believes that first there was a physical universe of matter and energy and eventually some of the matter in the universe came to life and grew to become conscious.

Having a mind and a body is one of the most fundamental experiences of being human. Perhaps that is the origin of the dilemma between idealism and materialism. Idealists believe that some form of mind or consciousness is primary in the universe and all of the material and sensual elements of reality are secondary. Materialists lean in the opposite direction. They see matter as the primary reality of the universe and mind as a secondary outgrowth of material interactions. The challenge for a materialist is to explain how life and consciousness appeared in a purely material universe. The challenge for an idealist is to explain the nature of the being out of which the physical universe manifests.

A strict materialist rejects the idea of some universal intelligence. They will demand that an idealist explain what kind of being the universal intelligence comes from, which is very hard to explain. Those of us who believe in a higher being have our own reasons for believing, but those reasons are intimate and personal. People have been trying to prove the existence of God for millennia and no one has succeeded yet.

On the other hand, an idealist wants to know where this physical universe came from. The materialist has a theory about a Big Bang out of which the whole universe emerged. The idealist wants to know how that is different from God. The idealist also wants to know how life and consciousness appeared in the universe. The materialist doesn't know that yet.

The point here is that neither the position of idealism or materialism can be definitively proven, but right now in the Western world, we live in a predominantly materialistic culture and so materialism has the benefit of the doubt. A thousand years ago almost everyone believed in God so that belief was given the benefit of the doubt. What this means is that today a materialist feels justified in demanding proof from an idealist for their belief, and the idealist tends to feel compelled to provide proof to justify what they believe. At the same time, it is largely acceptable for a materialist to be unable to explain something and not have their fundamental beliefs doubted as a result.

In a materialistic culture the idealist will always be frustrated in their attempts to prove their beliefs. That is because the standard for proof is being set by the dominant paradigm of materialism. The Idealist will have to find material proof that can be observed and measured because that is the only kind of proof that materialism accepts. Saying that you feel a deep love for divinity in your heart is not considered to be any legitimate proof even if it is your reason for believing what you do. Of course if you turn the question around and ask the materialist to prove that matter exists they will have an equally hard time. We don't generally ask for this kind of proof, because it just feels obvious that matter exists, but the reason that it feels obvious is because we have been taught to see it that way.

I am not introducing this line of reason to convince you that materialism is wrong and idealism is right. I don't know which is right. In fact, I don't believe that either is. I assume that the nature of reality is beyond my ability to comprehend or imagine. What I am trying to do is liberate you from the limitations of a materialistic paradigm. You don't have to disbelieve in materialism to be free from its limits. You only need to have a little doubt about it. You simply need to be a little unsure about it and introducing the perspective of Idealism helps, because it provides a powerful alternative explanation.

Think about this for a moment. Wherever you are, look at the world around you. Look at the room you're sitting in, or the landscape in front of you, feel the warmth or coldness of the air on your skin, listen to the sounds you hear all around you. If you think about it, the only world that exists is contained within your experience of the present moment. We imagine a world that exists beyond that. We imagine other places and other people that exist outside of our experience of the moment, but their existence is speculative rather than actual. This is why William James claimed that in reality we live in a world made of pure experience. We have ideas about the world beyond our immediate experience, but their reality cannot be verified. Again I want to reiterate that I am not trying to disprove the existence of the world beyond our immediate experience, I am simply offering a different way to think about things. If you focus on the world of your actual lived experience right now, rather than the conceptual world that you believe exists beyond your experience, something begins to happen. The world becomes immediate and magical. This is a shift in perspective that we will return to over and over again in this book. It is a shift out of a conceptualized reality and into an experiential one.

It's worth sitting with this point of view for a while. As a thought experiment you can have fun with this. For instance, what if the world ended at the edges of your experience? We assume that the world continues beyond what we can see. What if it doesn't? What if the edges of your experience are actually the edges of reality? What if nothing exists beyond our experience? That would make reality more like a dream than a physical place. In dreams we feel like we are living in a world that exists beyond our experience, but it doesn't. If someone sees me sleeping in bed while I'm dreaming they don't see the world of my dream. That world only exists in my mind, in consciousness. For thousands of years most people on Earth believed that the world that they lived in was a dream in the mind of God. God was the creator of the universe because she was the dreamer of the universe.

Now consider the possibility that you are living in a dream of your own creation. Maybe there isn't some universal God dreaming a big dream that we are all characters in. Maybe each of us is dreaming our own reality into existence. Every instant a countless number of simultaneously occurring events give birth to new worlds. And where do these worlds exist? They exist in the experience of the moment in which they were born.

This is how I visualize William James' conception of Radical Empiricism and Alfred North Whitehead's Process Philosophy. In both of these philosophies reality is seen not as a physical place but as an emergent phenomenon. Reality is not found in an external universe, but within the stream of consciousness of our own experience. If you imagine your consciousness as an ongoing flow of experience, that flow is reality. We live, as James put it, in a world of pure experience. Where a materialist sees physical particles as the fundamental building blocks of reality, James sees experience as the primary stuff. Let's think about this for a minute.

In the modern scientific paradigm we are taught that the universe began as an empty expanse of space filled with particles and energy, that emerged out of an initial burst. At that early stage there was no life and no consciousness in the universe. It was just an empty place with some physical stuff floating around in it. Gradually the stuff formed into stars, planets and, at least on this planet, life and consciousness. To our modern worldview reality existed before we got here. There was a real universe in place for trillions of years before there was anyone who could possibly have experienced it. For trillions of years the universe existed, although there were no living beings that could experience any part of it.

William James took exception to this. A universe that is not experienced, is not fully real. It does not constitute a full reality. Only an experienced universe is fully real. In his classic text, *The Varieties of Religious Experience*, James described a full fact of reality as containing, *"A conscious field, plus its object as felt or thought of, plus an attitude towards the object, plus the sense of a self to whom the attitude belongs…"* Let's break this down.

First of all a complete reality must be part of a conscious field, because no experience can exist in isolation. This is difficult to think about, but imagine something that exists in complete isolation. Such a thing cannot have any qualities, because if it were smooth, or sharp, or blue, or green, then it would not exist in isolation. It would exist with those qualities. So there would be at least two things in the field. Anything that exists completely alone does not truly exist. You might think about something existing all alone in an empty universe, but that thing wouldn't be all alone, it would be with an empty universe. Imagine something that existed in complete isolation, without any qualities, and without any space surrounding it. You can't imagine that. In order for something to exist it must exist in relation to something else. Alone, nothing exists.

So, reality must contain an object within a field of other

things, and then it must also be experienced. If there is an object in a field but there is no experience of it, then it doesn't really exist according to James. On top of this, the experience of the object must also contain an attitude towards it. There must be a feeling about it. I love this part of James' thinking. To be real, a thing can't just be experienced, there must be some feeling about it. Who or whatever is experiencing that object must also care. Before something can be considered real, it must be experienced, and also cared about. This makes care and concern an inherent part of realty. I love that. Finally reality has to include a sense of the self that experiences and cares.

Reality only comes into being when all of these pieces coexist. Think about your own experience right now. At any given moment, like the one you're living right now, your attention will be focused on something. You might be reading the words on this page, or thinking about what you just read in your mind. Or maybe your attention has wandered and you are thinking about what you will have for lunch, or looking at a tree outside your window. But, your attention is located somewhere right now. Notice what you are paying attention to. You know about this thing because of its relationship to other things that are part of your field of awareness. You know it is a tree because you can compare it with your memories of other trees. You know it is an oak tree because part of your conscious field is knowledge about the qualities of oak trees. You also have a feeling about the tree. Maybe you are appreciating its beauty. Or maybe you are annoyed that it is blocking your view of the ocean. And finally you have a sense of yourself as you look at the tree. You are aware that you are looking at a tree and feeling annoyed that you can't see the ocean behind it.

You are having a complete experience of this moment. A complete experience must include an experience of something that occurs in a context, a feeling about the object, and an awareness of yourself experiencing it. Each and every moment offers you a complete experience of reality. The complete experience of the present moment is the only world you are actually in contact with. The present moment is the only world you know. You might imagine a world beyond the experience of the present moment, but those are all ideas that exist in the experience of this moment. That is why William James asserted that this present moment is the only world that truly exists. When you experience this shift in perspective you suddenly feel dramatically connected to reality. Reality is no longer an idea. Reality is what you are experiencing right now. You realize that there is no longer anything separating you from reality. I have experienced this kind of radical immediacy many times and it is always thrilling.

Why does all this matter you ask? Good question. It matters because it is important to see how the reality we live in, exists inside the experiential reality of the present moment that we were just describing. As we look at the world around us we see an expanse of space filled with things. We imagine that we live on the surface of a round planet that floats in the infinite space of the universe. But that is not the world we live in, we live in the world of our experience of this moment, which is shaped by what we have been taught to believe about reality. We see reality as things that exist in space because we've been taught to interpret our experience in those terms. We don't know that reality is shaped that way, we only know we experience it that way.

When we speak about radical transformation we are talking about paradigm shifting. We are talking about a radical shift in the way we experience the present moment. Just a moment's reflection will reveal the value of this way of thinking. If we really live in a physical world full of things that float in infinite space, then that framework dramatically limits what's possible. But if we live in a world created from the experience of the present moment then almost anything can change. Going back to the dream metaphor, we see that anything can happen in dreams. If we live in an experiential reality that is more like a dream, then radical change is possible.

Over the past thirty years I have opened more and more deeply to the reality of the world of the present moment, and as I have, I've seen that not only can things in reality change, but the perceived nature of reality itself can shift. Over the years I've opened more and more to a world of infinite possibility. I say this not out of some naive belief that everything is possible, but because I realize that I don't know what's possible. And if you don't know what's possible, as I stated earlier, then effectively anything is. This wide open relationship to reality is the opportunity I'm sharing in this book. It offers the possibility of experiencing the profoundly malleable nature of reality itself. I want you to experience the ontological ground shift under your feet. I want you to realize that you don't actually know what's possible, or how much can actually change from one movement to the next. When you do, you will see that you have been living in just a thin slice of a multi-dimensional reality.

The possibility that reality might only exist in the experience of the present moment is very important to consider. As we've already said, we are taught that we live in an objective reality made of empty space and filled with physical things, and this reality existed as an objective fact long before we arrived in it. This means that the fundamental nature of reality is immune to our influence. Reality has been defined for us as exactly that part of existence that we have no affect over. We affect many of the things in reality, but reality itself we cannot touch. We assume that we have no influence over what is real.

As long as this assumption is unquestioned, then our spiritual experiences will always be forced to conform to our assumptions, or be dismissed as unreal. In the remainder of this book you will be introduced to a number of spiritual experiences I've had. These experiences didn't fit into our current understanding of reality, and so I had to step into an alternative reality in order to embrace the truth of them. The necessity to step into an alternative conception of reality is exactly what makes our spiritual experiences so transformative.

In this chapter we have been challenging some of the foundational assumptions of the current paradigm and setting the groundwork to begin to see that reality might be much more a creation of our minds than a physical place. This loosening up of our materialistic assumptions is necessary for those of us who want to open to the radical visions of reality that our spiritual and mystical experiences reveal. Many of us have spiritual experiences but we don't just have them, we also interpret them. The way we interpret our spiritual revelations is just as important as having them in the first place, because how we interpret them will have a direct effect on how transformative they are for us. The way we interpret our spiritual experiences can create a new reality for us. I am writing this book to explore this interpretive aspect of spiritual breakthrough and radical transformation. As we look at a variety of different types of spiritual experiences we will creatively explore how they can be interpreted and how our sense of reality changes, or not, as a result. I don't intend to tell you what the nature of reality is. I simply want to expand your capacity to imagine new possibilities and show you how that increases the transformative potential of the spiritual experiences you do have.

CHAPTER THREE

Inner Freedom

"And I, I myself, am the center that exists only because the geometry of the abyss demands it; I am the nothing around which all this spins, I exist so that it can spin, I am a center that exists only because every circle has one."

- Fernando Pessoa

HOPEFULLY YOU ARE INSPIRED ABOUT the importance of this conversation so now we can start to dive into the specifics of some of my own spiritual experiences and how I have interpreted them. You will see that my journey has left me with a vision of how spiritual transformation occurs and the role that the creative interpretation of our mystical experiences plays in that process. The first thing we need to explore is spiritual liberation. That means the radical release of the constraints that keep our inner spirit from soaring to its ultimate and full potential.

My work supports the liberation of the human spirit. That means freeing the energy and intelligence that animates your heart, mind, and body so that it can manifest its full potential in your life. If we look at this from a personal point of view we could say that we are liberating the energy of life so that it is more available to you, and through you to the world. Spiritual liberation from this perspective means that the creative source of the cosmos begins to fuel and guide your life, and when more people are guided by that ultimate creative source, we will live in a new world.

I have experienced the liberation of my spirit as a deep and dramatic emotional release. My heart burst wide open, and my mind became magnificently clear and sensitive. For months afterward I was continually flooded with seemingly boundless energy and passion for life.

If we look at the experience of inner freedom and interpret its possible meaning from a universal perspective we see that something profound is happening. The cosmic energy that is the ultimate source of all the love, wisdom and conscious awareness in this universe is being liberated to manifest itself freely through us. This is how I see spiritual liberation. It is not our liberation. It is the liberation of the cosmic energy of life itself. It is the freedom of the universe.

Here is where we have to stop and think. I am making some big claims. I have come to these conclusions over decades and I have no doubt about them, even though I know I can't prove them to you, and I am well aware they could be, and probably are in many significant ways, wrong. When I experienced spiritual liberation, was I really experiencing the liberation of the energetic source of life? Or was I imagining that I was? This is exactly the question we have to ask. We need to explore to what extent the meaning of our spiritual experiences is a reflection of some objective reality? And to what extent they are purely imagined. And most interestingly, to what degree is all of reality always purely imagined.

Let's start with the facts as best as I can relate them to you. I already told you about the realization I had about the inherent risk of being alive and the possibility of dedicating myself to living a spiritual life. That happened during a spiritual talk that I attended and it opened me up dramatically. Of course, after that night I went home, to an ordinary life, and there was no way to reconcile what I had just experienced with the life that I was living. This is what happens to almost everyone. You have a spiritual experience, it reveals something extraordinary about what is possible for your life, but more often than not, you are living a life that is not a reflection of that possibility.

We all start out living life as best we can. We learn about life from our culture and the lessons of our personal experience. The lives we live end up being a reflection of the values and assumptions of our culture. Look at people's lives. There are certainly many differences, but if we step back we will see that the vast majority of human lives within a culture are very similar. There is a certain form of life that is supported by that culture and it is the rare individual that strays too far from it. So when we liberate ourselves from the inner restraints that have shaped us, we wake up in a life that was formed by the restraints we have just shed. We land back in our life and find that it doesn't fit anymore.

After that night, when I saw clearly that all human lives are an equal risk and that a spiritual life was a real possibility for me, I landed back in a life where I was married to a beautiful woman who was deeply spiritual, but didn't have the same interests that I now had. And I was working in a career as an engineer that no longer felt like me. I didn't have spiritually minded friends. I felt like I was in the wrong life. This is the situation that most finders end up in. They find something that changes everything in terms of their vision of what's possible, but they are faced with the hard work of changing the life they are currently living.

For a year I tried to make it all work together. I became more and more involved with the teacher and community that I had found. I tried to include my wife in my new spiritual life in every way that I could think of. Still, it eventually became clear that the path I was on just wasn't hers. It was time for me to do the unthinkable and end our marriage. To understand what a difficult and monumental decision this was for me, you have to know a little bit about my background.

Three of my grandparents were born in Portugal and emigrated to the United States at a young age. My remaining grandmother was born in the United States, but her father and mother also emigrated from Portugal. So I was raised as a Portuguese second generation American, and that meant that above all, family was the most important thing. My aunt divorced her husband and my memory was that no one in the family talked with her or her children for almost a decade.

I had come to realize that if we stayed together, then neither my wife nor I would be able to live the life we wanted to live. In the moment that I was getting ready to tell her that I thought we should get a divorce, all of my cultural and personal conditioning rose up with a vengeance. As I sat getting ready to speak I felt a deafening scream in my ears. It was as if someone was screaming "no" as loudly as they could in both of my ears. I was very resolved that I had to go through with this, in spite of the fact that I was certain that I would be condemned and blackballed by everyone I knew.

Very slowly and deliberately I spoke. "I don't think we can stay married" was the only sentence I could muster, and given how much we had both been aware of the situation that was enough. As I breathed in the air to speak that sentence the "No" in my head grew louder. By the time the words came out of my mouth, I could only feel them rolling over my tongue. I couldn't hear them at all because the internal scream was deafening. As soon as the words had left my inner world and entered the shared space between me and my wife the screaming stopped. Everything became completely silent. A deep sense of calm came over me and a huge burden was lifted off my body.

It was as if I had been living my life wearing a straitjacket made of heavy metal. I was bound up, constrained from moving and so heavily burdened that I could hardly walk. The straitjacket was emotional, not physical, built up over time, constructed out of all the ideas that kept me tightly identified with being the person I had come to know as Jeff. These ideas dictated what I was capable of, and what I was not capable of, what I liked and what I didn't like, what I could do, and what I couldn't do. Effectively these ideas kept me endlessly looping through patterns of thought and behavior that were familiar to me. Getting a divorce was way outside of this familiar set of behaviors and so the entire edifice of my personal identity was being challenged.

When the straitjacket fell away I felt like I was floating in midair. I literally thought I had lifted off the chair I was sitting on. I had never felt so light and free. In that moment I learned what the phrase *lightness of being* means. I was free. Free from the constraint of limiting beliefs. My heart was bursting with joy. I started laughing out loud. It struck me as so funny that it had been so easy to let go of it all. It had only taken a moment of courage to drop all of the limiting ideas that had me bound up as tight as a drum. I laughed out loud so hard that my belly started to hurt. I felt like I was in on the big cosmic joke. Freedom was always ours for the taking. All we had to do was step out beyond our fears and our spirit would be liberated. I laughed and laughed until my stomach hurt so badly I had to stop.

Once I stopped laughing, it occurred to me that even though it had been so easy to drop all those limiting ideas, it had still taken me decades to do it, and there were billions of people on the planet that would never discover the secret. They would live with the burden of limiting beliefs for the rest of their lives and many would simply die never knowing what it feels like to be free. This realization made me so sad that I cried and cried and cried, sobbing so hard that my stomach started hurting again. Eventually my stomach hurt so badly that I couldn't continue, and I stopped, but then the hilarity of how easy it would be for everyone to just let go struck me and I started laughing again.

I cycled back and forth between hysterical laughing and inconsolable crying about six or seven times. When it was over, I felt totally exhausted, utterly drained, and completely free. I saw my life ahead as an unwritten book and there were no more rules telling me what was possible. I felt utter exhilaration and fully responsible for whatever the outcome of my life would be. I was no longer living under any constraints, and I could no longer blame anyone or anything that went wrong. My life was now in my own hands, a matter of conscious choice.

I continued to float on air for the next six months. I never felt like my feet touched the ground during all that time. I glided through life, not just physically but emotionally and also spiritually. Nothing bothered me. Even the most challenging circumstances were met with a sense of inner calm and equanimity. I also found that my perceptions had changed dramatically. I seemed to be able to see through things into their inner workings. When it came to people, this meant that I was starting to be able to read their minds. I would see little emotional thought bubbles in their stomachs that would then slowly move upward. As they got closer to the mouth they took on a more definite shape and I could start to guess what they were about to say. Then I would see the thought bubble burst through someone's mouth as words and I was uncannily accurate in predicting what was about to be said.

It is impossible to explain how miraculous and utterly life altering those six months were for me. My life was never the same. I had stepped out of the reality I had been living in and into a new one. I had no idea where I was going, but I was on my way.

I have just related to you a story in terms of the facts. I described things that I actually experienced. There is minimal interpretation. Of course, even in this description there is some interpretation going on. For instance, when I say that my heart was bursting with joy, that is an interpretation. I was clearly feeling something, and it felt to me like joy, but still that is an interpretation. Even more so, when I talk about feeling liberated from a straitjacket of limiting beliefs, there is a lot of interpretation going on. The point is, even when we are trying to be merely factual in our explanations of things, we are still interpreting events to some extent.

If you think about the experience that I described having for six months, you can probably imagine that I spent a lot of time thinking about what was happening to me. Explosive breakthroughs and dramatic shifts in our perception, are not just events that we passively accept. Confronted with such a different experience of reality we cannot help but feel compelled to understand what is happening to us, why it is happening, and what it means. Just about everyone who experiences spiritual revelation will try to understand what has happened and why. When we engage in speculation about our revelatory experiences, we are attempting to find an interpretation of them that somehow makes sense to us. This is why two people can have exactly the same experience and yet interpret what is happening in completely different ways. And this is one of the main points of this book: the way we interpret our revelatory experiences will determine what effect they have, or do not have, on our lives. Some interpretations will lead to massive change, others to none at all.

My initial interpretation of this liberating breakthrough experience was psychological. At the time I had not been deeply steeped in spiritual philosophy, but I had been studying psychology. Using that lens to interpret through. I came to the conclusion that the lightness I felt was due to the release of emotional constraints and limiting beliefs. It made sense to me that over time I had been told things about myself that I believed, and I had experienced things that had shaped my emotional responses to life. Because I had taken a step in direct conflict with my existing belief system, I had somehow shattered the grip that my beliefs and emotional reactions had on me. I believed that the intense emotional response that I had was some kind of recalibration of my nervous system around my new found state of freedom. It seemed to me that emotions that had been trapped in my body were being released all at once. It was as if a big knot inside me had been untied and everything was now free to flood out. When I was done emoting, I felt drained and limp. It was as if all of the tension in my body was gone. I felt soft and lighter than air.

At the time that I had this experience I had been meditating for a few years, but the context for my practice was more psychological than spiritual. I had been studying cognitive science, which is the science of how we perceive and understand the world. My psychological life was a fairly recent discovery for me and I was fascinated by it. When I experienced this dramatic opening it was only natural for me to explain it to myself in terms of the psychology I had been learning about.

Of course, the experience also happened in a spiritual context, because my decision to leave my marriage was the direct result of the time I spent with a spiritual teacher. For this reason, I also interpreted this experience as a spiritual experience in which my energy had been released from constraints and was now flowing freely. I thought of this experience as the experience of spiritual freedom, which to me at the time meant that the energy of my true being had been liberated.

The psychological part of my interpretation allowed this experience to fit fairly comfortably in my existing worldview. It was a very strange experience to be sure, but it did not seem to violate the accepted beliefs about human psychology. The ways that I interpreted the experience as a spiritual breakthrough meant that it stood as a profound confirmation for my desire to leave my current life and pursue a spiritual one. And because I associated this experience directly with the teacher I had been working with, it gave me the courage to join his community. I would say, in general, the psychological aspect of the interpretation allowed me to embrace, and not reject, what had happened, while the spiritual aspect allowed me to make changes in my life as a result.

If I had not had the psychological interpretation, the whole thing might have seemed too weird to even accept. If I had not had the spiritual interpretation, it may not have given me the courage to join a spiritual community. When we have a spiritual experience, we are always experiencing something beyond our current understanding. We will always feel compelled to try to understand it by interpreting its meaning. I believe that it is possible to be more conscious about how we interpret these experiences. Some ways of interpreting our breakthrough experiences will allow us to both embrace what has happened, while at the same time giving us the courage to change our lives as a result. If we can't find an interpretation that allows us to embrace the experience, we will dismiss it as unreal. If we can't find an interpretation that gives us the courage to change as a result, then the experience will simply become a memory of a very strange yet ultimately inconsequential episode that happened to us.

Only when the way we interpret our breakthrough experiences allows us to both accept the reality of them and have the courage to change, will they result in real transformation and growth. This book is a contemplation about how spiritual experiences can be interpreted and an exploration of some specific ways that I have interpreted my own breakthrough experiences.

It will be important right now to tackle the elephant in the room. Namely, the feeling you are probably having about the fact that you can't just make up an interpretation of something and pretend it is true. If these things that happen to us are real, then we have to find out what they really are, not just make up a story about them. This is the kind of thought that will stop us from consciously participating in the interpretation of our experience, but here's the thing - *all of reality is interpreted.* That means if we don't consciously take responsibility for how we interpret reality, then we are most likely leaving that interpretation in the hands of unconscious beliefs and cultural norms.

The point is that we are interpreting reality all of the time, mostly unconsciously, anyway. I am suggesting that we can take conscious responsibility for how we interpret our spiritual experiences so that we maximize their benefit in our lives. I know this sounds sacrilegious, but that is only because of the unconscious way we have learned to think about reality. As I have already explained, we have been taught that reality is a physical place full of material things, that was here before we were. Within this belief system, every real thing must be understood in terms of the material universe and the limits of what can exist within it. The idea that we can interpret reality and that our interpretations could influence what is real, does not fit into that paradigm.

But this is exactly how I have come to see it. And if you think about it for a minute, it makes sense. I knew someone who trained his dog with an electric fence. The electric fence was a wire that delivered an electric shock when the dog touched it. The wire was wrapped around the yard and over the course of a few months, the dog learned not to go near it. Even though the dog couldn't see it, he learned to stay clear. Once the dog stopped going near the fence, it was taken down. The dog would never cross that boundary again. From a materialistic worldview, we would say the reality is that there is no more fence. But from the point of view of the dog's capacity to function, it certainly appeared as if the fence remained. So the question arises, should we define reality based on material presence, or functional effect? Materially there was no fence, but functionally it was there, even if it only existed in the mind of the dog.

There are different ways to think about reality, or different dimensions to what is real. I once attended a lecture by an Italian philosopher who wanted to change the way we understood the reality of who we are. In a materialistic paradigm, we understand ourselves to be an organism defined by the existence of our bodies. When this body ceases to function we imagine that we cease to exist. We will be considered dead by those around us. The Italian philosopher thought it would be better if we defined ourselves not in terms of our physical existence, but in terms of our effect on others. That means that Leonardo DaVinci is still alive, because his paintings are still affecting people. It also means that I am not only located here where I am typing. I am also there with you, wherever you are, while you read these words. Defining ourselves in terms of our physical existence feels right because we are taught that it is right, but ultimately, it is just a convention, an interpretation, that we have learned to adopt. The idea that we can create reality by how we interpret our experience feels wrong because we have been taught that it is wrong, but that is also an interpretation that has become convention. In this book I am going to ask you to adopt a different convention. I am not telling you that this new way of seeing reality is the only right way. I simply want you to experiment with it and come to your own conclusions.

I want you to imagine that reality is constantly being created, at least in part, by our interpretations of it. That means that how we imagine things are, actually helps shape how they show up for us, and also what effect they have on us. When my friend imagined that his spiritual opening was just a weird anomaly in his life *it became* just a weird anomaly in his life, and so it had little effect on him. When I imagined that my spiritual opening was a calling to live in devotion to spirituality alone, it became that calling, and totally transformed my life. In our current paradigm we would say that since the two experiences had different effects they must not have been the same experience. I want you to consider that they were exactly the same experience, just interpreted differently. They became different in the reality of our lives because they were interpreted differently. The interpretation of our experience becomes the reality of it.

Now I want to share how I have ultimately interpreted the experience of spiritual liberation that I had the day I told my wife that I didn't think we could remain married. I no longer think of the emotional upheavals I experienced that day exclusively in terms of my own psycho-spiritual freedom. I have come to adopt a much more expansive interpretation of what happened. I don't even think of it as something that happened to me any more. I think of it as something that happened in the cosmos. The interpretation that I'm about to share will give you a fundamental sense of how I have come to see reality more and generally, and again, I am not sharing it because I know it is true. I have no doubt about it, but I don't want you to take my word for it. I want you to explore it. Take it for a test drive and see how it fits.

I believe that the conscious awareness that we all experience as our awareness is actually coming from the cosmos itself. We are part of a conscious universal being in the same way that our eyes or our mouth are a part of us. We are not a separate thing that exists in a dead three dimensional space, we are not even a separate thing that exists in a living universal being. We are an aspect, a feature, a living part of a living universe. We are not separate from the world around us, we are a part of it. We are not separate from reality, we are part of it. Our thoughts about reality are part of reality. The way we understand things to be, is a part of what they are. We are not aware of a universe that is separate from us. Our awareness does not even belong to us. It belongs to the universe.

Right now I am looking at my computer screen while I type these words. I'm looking at the screen with my eyes, but it is not my eyes that see the screen, it is me that sees it. My eyes are a part of me. If my eyes were removed from my body they would not see anything. In the same way, the universe is experiencing through me. I'm not having this experience, the universe is having it. I am the organ of perception, not the perceiver. This is how I interpret myself in the cosmos. This is not congruent with the paradigm of scientific materialism which understands a human being to be an organism that exists in a universe that it is fundamentally separate from.

I also want to say that awareness is not something that exists in the universe in any way that could be considered separate from it. Awareness is the very essence of the universe. At the most fundamental level we live in awareness. We imagine ourselves to be an organism that is aware because it has awareness. We believe that the awareness we have is a part of us, a characteristic of us. We naturally apply this understanding even to the idea of a living universe and so saying that the universe is aware might still sound like there is a physical universe of three dimensional space that has awareness as a characteristic. That is not what I mean. The universe is awareness. There is no universe separate from awareness. This makes the universe more like a dream. My interpretation of reality tends to be philosophically idealistic. I see reality as fundamentally mental, not material. It is like a dream. What is a dream made of? Awareness, consciousness, and experience, nothing more. A dream is not made up of atoms, molecules, rocks and other stuff. A dream is made out of pure experience. I believe that reality is also made of pure experience.

I started on the spiritual path for personal psycho-spiritual reasons. I was motivated by a desire for personal freedom. I wanted to transcend the constraints of limiting beliefs and emotional patterns so that I could realize my full potential as a human being. As I progressed along the path of awakening I discovered the larger life of the cosmos. The spiritual experiences that I had, some of which are described in this book, revealed to me that the universe had a life of its own and that I was a part of that. I saw that the cosmos wanted to live through me. It wanted to gain access to the world of time and space with me as a vehicle. I saw that the spiritual path was not about my liberation as an individual and separate human being, it was about the liberation of cosmic awareness through me, into the world. At this point I developed a passionate desire to get out of the way so that the higher Self of the universe could find its way to the world through me.

I believe that the promise of spiritual life is the realization of our highest potential for bringing more love and goodness into existence. None of us knows for sure what that life will look like for us, but if we surrender our lives to the energy that animates the cosmos then that source of compassionate wisdom will optimize our lives. The challenge we face in living a spiritual life, is that at the start we are already surrendered to something else

– the fears, desires and concerns of the separate sense of self and the paradigm it was conditioned by. Our experience of ourselves and the world is shaped by the deeply held beliefs of the current paradigm and those beliefs must be uprooted, reevaluated and ultimately revised or discarded in order for us to liberate the cosmic energy that flows through us.

We have not been trained to see the universe as a living conscious being. We have been taught to see it as a vacuous expanse of empty space filled with material things. And we have learned to see ourselves as a physical organism that has itself become consciously aware. These materialistic assumptions about ourselves are foundational to the dominant paradigm. These beliefs limit our potential because they act as filters and lenses that determine what is possible and what is not. These assumed limitations are exactly what the love and wisdom of the cosmos wants to be liberated from. The universal source of energy that animates your being wants to express its full potential. Our own personal desire to live our full potential is a reflection of this universal desire for wholeness. We reflect the universe's passion for fulfillment like a mirror reflects the light from the Sun. Our spiritual passion is not ours alone. It belongs to a universal being that wants to be free and unimpeded. We are that being.

As we continue on this journey, you will see that this is the grand narrative that shapes the way I interpret my own existence and that interpretation in turn shapes the nature and purpose of my spiritual experiences. When we liberate ourselves from the fears and desires of the separate self, we immediately begin to express a profound depth of love, wisdom and sensitivity. The lifeforce energy of the cosmos is now guiding our lives. When this happens, our hearts, minds, bodies and spirits become available to be moved by the universal source. Let's take another look at the experience of spiritual liberation that I described earlier, this time from a cosmic perspective.

Remember, I am not telling you the truth about reality. This is my interpretation of it, and It is one that other people share, but it is an interpretation nonetheless. The essential nature of the cosmos is a universal being. That being is a kind of self. Not a self that has a body or a face, but a self that has feelings, ideas, concerns and desires of its own. How do I know this? Because my spiritual experiences have revealed it to me over and over again. It is the interpretation that makes the most sense of my experience. I have no doubt about the reality of this vision, and I am aware that the fact that I interpret reality this way is shaping the way reality shows up. If I had interpreted things differently, a different experience of reality would have resulted.

This all gets very loopy. Our interpretations of reality shape our experience of reality, and that experience in turn convinces us of the reality of our interpretations. It may sound like I am just making stuff up and then convincing myself that it is true. The ideas that I'm sharing may sound wildly speculative to you, but I want to remind you that even if our interpreted reality is conventional and shared by everyone around us, it is still in-terpreted. Everyone thought the world was flat for thousands of years. Because they believed that, they saw a flat earth. That interpretation has been discarded. What I am saying in this book is that our current interpretation of reality is almost definitely not final. It too will be discarded and replaced with something else. Since we know that our current interpretation of reality is not final and not ultimately true, why not be creative and think for ourselves?

Continuing on with my own interpretation of reality, I want to say that the cosmic being is the source of my being. I am that cosmic being, and so are you. That being is the source of the awareness that we all experience as our own. It is the dreamer of this reality and it is all the people in the dream. The universe began as a dream of reality and at some point the dream took the shape that we experience now. It is a dream of a universe of infinite space filled with material things that interact. It is a dream about a planet upon which life developed and through one species of life on that planet a form of consciousness that we call human developed. In this dream the human beings that exist, almost unanimously agree that the conscious awareness they experience is being generated inside themselves. It is their consciousness. They possess it. They believe that their consciousness came into existence on the day that they were born and will cease to be on the day they die. It is a dream about a planet full of people who believe that they are independently conscious entities all separate from each other and from the universe they find themselves in.

The cosmic source wants to wake up through this species. It wants to recognize itself through these people. They have forgotten their universal nature and the unity of their being. They have forgotten that each individual consciousness comes from the same source. They have forgotten who they truly are. The cosmos wants to remember itself through these people. It wants all people to drop the sense of separation and division so that the true source of their being will be revealed. This passion for Self-realization presses up through the consciousness of every individual all the time. Some individuals feel this passion, identify it as their own personal passion for self-realization, and begin a spiritual search.

Once on the spiritual path the universal source pushes against all of the ideas that block it from flowing freely. It pushes against our cultural beliefs and our personal fears and desires. It pushes against all of the blocks and distortions that have resulted from the ways we have been hurt in our lives. It pushes against our doubts and uncertainties. The universal desire for Self-realization also attempts to redirect our passions and energies. It inspires us in directions that will liberate us more fully. It calls us in one direction and then another. That energy is always with us, breaking through our resistances and guiding us forward toward deeper realization and spiritual freedom.

If we surrender to the guidance of this universal energy it will overtake us. Only when we stop trying to guide our own awakening do we become available to be truly carried forward by the higher being of the cosmos. Any effort that we make to guide ourselves forward will inevitably be a source of limitation. We cannot envision who we truly are. Any ideas we have about it will inevitably be partial. In order to become truly available we must give up, let go, and surrender everything we think we know about ourselves, reality and the spiritual journey to higher selfhood. Only when we become innocent like a child are we ready to be moved by spirit.

The day when I told my wife that I didn't think that we should remain married, I stepped beyond every idea that I had about myself and life and stepped into an unknown future. Those ideas and the emotional guard rails they represented kept me on a straight and narrow track safely wrapped up in the identity of being Jeff and all that that implied. Suddenly I stepped outside of myself. I had done something so unthinkable that I no longer knew who I was or what I was capable of.

But at a deeper level something more profound had occurred. The cosmic passion for universal liberation and Higher Self Discovery had broken through the constraints of my former small self identity. That energy was now free to flow through me. I was experiencing the incredible miracle of being an open vehicle for a higher being, but more importantly, through me, that universal being now had another foothold in this world. I imagine a universal being, having created a universe, desperately wanting to enter it. That higher being sees its creation from the outside. It sees some of the creatures waking up to consciousness, but not realizing that they are one with the creator. Occasionally some of those creatures step out of the conditioned pattern of their identity and become free and available.

A liberated human being is someone who is no longer compelled by normal human concerns. They have woken up, at least partially, to their true identity as an aspect of the cosmic being that gave birth to this universe in the first place. This is the start of a new spiritual journey. The spiritual journey begins when a small 's' self, an individual human identity, experiences an awakening to its own higher possibilities. The journey that unfolds from that point leads to the gradual, or sudden, release of the constraints of that identity. At that point the individual human being becomes available to be guided by a higher 'S' Self, a cosmic being if you will. The next stage of the spiritual journey has begun.

The second stage of the spiritual journey involves small 's' Jeff, but it isn't his journey. It is the journey of the awakening of the cosmic being. Jeff may have all kinds of ideas about himself and his awakening, but ultimately there is something much bigger going on. The larger journey of cosmic awakening cannot be seen from within the limits of a human point of view. As a human being we can only see a tiny fraction of the totality of what is. Imagine someone who lived in a small room without any windows. That person noticed that periodically light would shine through the cracks between the boards in the wall illuminating the room. But the only world they knew was that small room without windows. They might speculate all day long about the nature of that light that periodically provided the only dim illumination of their life, but the chances of them guessing correctly at the true nature of the world outside or the Sun that illuminated the sky, would be nearly zero.

Similarly, we cannot begin to guess the nature of the journey of awakening that opens up for the cosmic being once it has access to our lives. We are swept along on that journey, we even participate in it, but we cannot begin to fathom its true depth and breadth. Our participation in that cosmic awakening will have profound and wonderful effects on us and our lives, but those are a byproduct of the journey, not the point. If we get too caught up in what that journey means about us and how we can control and direct it, we will once again become an impediment to the larger journey that needs only our surrender.

There is a paradox that must be lived in the second phase of the spiritual journey. On the one hand all that is required is our surrender. We don't need to know anything about that journey and it is best if we stop trying to understand it at all. Our speculations will never be able to grasp the full magnitude of what's happening and to the extent that they start to shape our actions, they are likely to be misleading. At the same time, we are meaning making creatures and most of us cannot avoid making meaning out of our spiritual experiences. There have always been those rare spiritual realizers who opened to the cosmic being and simply surrendered without any need to understand what was happening. This may be the ideal, but it seems to be an exceedingly rare attainment.

The rest of us will consciously or unconsciously interpret our spiritual experiences, and those interpretations will affect how they unfold in our lives. The premise of this book is that it is better for us to be conscious about our interpretations than simply to allow unconscious cultural and personal habits of perception to interpret them for us. I have come to my current interpretation of my spiritual journey after decades of dedicated practice. I am utterly convinced about them, and I am aware that they are interpretations that will inevitably prove to be as limited as I am. The reason I am sharing them with you is not because I know they are true. It is because they have been so extremely beneficial to my own spiritual journey that I believe there will be others like you who may receive the same benefit that I have.

I believe that on the day when I told my wife that I didn't think we could be married, the energy of an awakening cosmos was unleashed, and everything that has happened to me spiritually since that day has been a direct result. Jeff has a story and a history of personal awakening. That story is real and it is important to Jeff and those that are touched by him, but it is not the whole story. The bigger story is the story of a universe awakening to itself through vehicles like you and me who have, to some degree or other, surrendered to a larger journey of awakening.

CHAPTER FOUR

Constant Consciousness

*"We are not human beings having a spiritual experience;
we are spiritual beings having a human experience."*

- Pierre Teilhard de Chardin

IN THE LAST CHAPTER WE spoke about an experience of emotional release that can easily be interpreted within the current paradigm. The experience I want to describe next, is not so easy to see through that lens. In fact the only current paradigm interpretation of the experience I'm about to recount, would be that it was the result of a chemical imbalance in the brain that occurred from so much meditation. Before we get into that, there is a little more I want to say about the overarching way I see reality.

There are two philosophical terms that are important for us to understand, pluralism and relativism. These two terms are often used interchangeably, but to my understanding there is a subtle, but very important distinction between them.

Pluralism is the belief that reality is made up of more than one fundamental element. This idea stands in opposition to Monism which is the belief that reality is made up of only one fundamental element. A strict Idealist is a monist who believes that reality is made up of only mind and that the solidity of matter is only an experience of our minds. A strict materialist is a monist who believes that reality is made up of only matter and that the experience of consciousness is produced by the electro-chemical activity of the brain.

As I have already stated, the philosopher William James believed that reality is made up of pure experience like a dream.

This made him an idealist of sorts, but not in the most traditional sense. James called himself a pluralist, because he didn't believe that reality was a single dream that we are all a part of. He saw reality as being composed of individual instances of experience. Each instance of experience that I have, or you have, or anyone has, is adding more stuff to reality. James was actually an anti-idealist in the sense that he did not believe that there was some universal mind that was dreaming the dream of reality. He believed that only individual instances of experience were real. He saw us living in a reality that was multiple. He didn't want to use the word universe, because it implied one, he wanted to call it a pluralverse, implying many.

If we think about a beach, we might say that the beach was made up of sand, as if sand was one thing. From a pluralistic point of view we would argue that the beach is not made up of sand, but rather of individual grains of sand. Each grain of sand is equally as real as any other. To James, nothing existed outside of individual instances of experience. The word sand is an abstract category that refers to the collection of individual grains. Similarly James would say that the word experience is an abstract name for the collection of all individual instances of experience. What we call reality always occurs within these individual instances of experience. If you want to throw another philosophical term into the pot, we could say that James was a nominalist because he believed that only individual instances or reality are truly real. To a nominalist there are only individual actual horses, there the idea of a horse is not a real thing, it is just an idea. Pluralism, at least the way James defined it, is a belief that reality is multiple and completely contained within individual instances of experience.

Relativism is something different. Relativism is the conviction that no truth about reality is ever universal. All understanding of truth is relative to some context or point of view. No truth is always true everywhere, because all truth is relative. To a strict relativist nothing is absolutely true because all truth is determined within some set of influencing factors. The meaning of anything is always dependent on the context in which it is being considered. Things do not have inherent meaning, significance and value. Meaning, significance and value is always relative to context. Water is one thing after you just finished drinking a liter of it, and it is something else entirely if you have been walking for three days in the desert without any. Meaning is not fixed, it is relative. Relativism stands in opposition to Absolutism. Absolutism is the belief that at least some things have a meaning and significance that is inherent in them and cannot be altered. This means that they are true independently from any context, which means they hold true in all contexts.

People often see the positions of relativism and pluralism as inevitably believing in nihilism, which is the belief that nothing is true. The implied logic goes like this. "If you believe that reality is made up of many things and those things do not have inherent meaning, then nothing is really real, and you will inevitably slip into the apathetic conviction that nothing matters." I understand that there is a real concern here, but it is not necessarily the case. And I believe that for us to surrender to the larger spiritual journey of the cosmic being we must find a way to authentically embrace a form of pluralism that does not imply relativism or nihilism. This means that we must find a way to accept that reality is made up of individual instances of experience, and that they are all equally, or at least potentially equally, real. We must give ourselves the benefit of choosing between realities as our spiritual experiences present them to us. That means we must be less rigidly attached to the reality that already is, so that we remain open to stepping into a new one as soon as the opportunity presents itself. We must recognize that we live in a pluralverse that is made up of many instances of experience that are all doorways to a new lived experience of reality.

To expand my own thinking in this way I have adopted a

multi-dimensional view of reality. In order to enter into a new paradigm of being we will need to make room for reality to be weirder and more bizarre than we would generally feel comfortable with. To me this means embracing the reality of a universe that exists in many dimensions of being simultaneously. All these dimensions are equally real, but only a small handful of them are currently visible to us. These dimensions pass through, cross over, and affect each other in ways that we cannot imagine. We occasionally see these trans-dimensional intersections as inexplicable synchronicities without realizing what they actually tell us about how reality works.

In addition to teaching meditation and spiritual philosophy, I write novels. My novels are fundamentally vehicles for expressing the multi-dimensional nature of reality in stories, and so I call the type of fiction I write transdimensional fiction. This book will sound more like fiction than fact to some people, but that is part of my point. I believe that reality is more like a piece of fiction that we co-author than it is a collection of objective facts that are given to us to deal with.

In an early book of mine called Radical Inclusivity, I acknowledged my belief that our being is not limited to only the three dimensions of space and time that we are familiar with. We exist in many dimensions of reality simultaneously even if we cannot perceive them. Each of our actions affect dimensions of reality that are invisible to us, and things that occur in those dimensions are always affecting our reality as well. I believe that we are part of an unending multi-dimensional feedback loop of overlapping influence. Reality is relentlessly shifting and fluctuating in more dimensions than we can imagine, and those fluctuations are affecting the reality of all other dimensions.

So, what are we?

Amid this field of multiple dimensions of realities, we emerge as a perceptual convergence of awareness that solidifies briefly into a self-determined identity calling itself human. We are a locus of awareness that appears to have attached itself to a biological organism. That organism provides the center that any source for awareness needs to be stable.

As I read the last few sentences I wonder if anyone will be able to understand what I am trying to say, and even more I wonder if what I am trying to say makes any sense. Regardless, it is what I believe, and it is the vision that drives my life and my work. The spiritual experiences that I have had, have led me gradually but unerringly to this interpretation of reality and now this overarching interpretation shapes the way I perceive all my experience. What I want you to see is how our perception of reality is shaped by a continual feedback loop. Energies from unseen dimensions are constantly streaming through the dimensions of our familiar perception. These energies affect what happens here and at the same time whatever is happening here affects these higher dimensional energies as they pass by. As these energies move on to other dimensional realities, they create change there as well. This loop continues as all the many dimensions of reality affect each other toward some higher end.

We are not an organism that exists on the surface of a single planet, or rather we are not only an organism that exists on the surface of a single planet. We are a multi-dimensional 'beingness' that exists throughout all dimensions. We have no edges or limits. Our existence extends infinitely in all dimensions of being. We exist in the pluralverse not like a flower that sits in a vase in a room. We exist like the scent of a flower that spreads throughout the room. We are not locatable anywhere in particular, the scent of our being exists everywhere always.

We have become temporarily limited by the awareness that appears to have become identified with the lifespan of one particular organism living on the surface of a single planet. That awareness has generated a story about itself that it has come to believe is the totality of what it is. We have forgotten our Higher Cosmic Selfhood. Our spiritual experiences challenge the limits of our individual self-concept. In these moments we open to possibilities that simply could not be possible as an independent consciousness generating self. Confronted with such a challenging opening we either need to dismiss it as unreal and forget about it, or dramatically alter our understanding of reality to accommodate it. This demand is what gives our spiritual experiences their transformative power. They insist that we transform to accommodate them, or lose access to the world they reveal to us.

The realization of our multi-dimensional existence is an opportunity to relax into our true Self and accept responsibility for the invisible affects we have in all dimensions. At the same time, we have the chance to grow in sensitivity so that we can begin to see and feel the previously invisible influences that are affecting us from dimensions beyond. I believe that it is possible to live into the fullness of who we are. Currently, we are moving through a localized constraint of identity that has captivated our attention, temporarily. Our desire to embrace and acclimate to our wildest spiritual experiences is part of the bigger spiritual journey of the awakening cosmos. That desire to move past our current constriction is coming from the whole of reality, not just from a few organisms of a single species, on one planet. The cosmic energy of consciousness is currently caught in a story about being members of a self-aware species on a planet called Earth. And we have the monumental opportunity to release that cosmic energy from its current limits. We are an infinite being having multi-dimensional effects beyond our comprehension. The effects of the choices we make are not limited to what we can perceive or imagine. Our thoughts, feelings, and actions are rippling out into the vast expanse of a multi-dimensional cosmos of which we are both a single aspect and the whole of.

OK, so now you know what I think about who we are. I mentioned earlier that I write novels in a self-created genre that I call transdimensional fiction. I started writing novels because

I felt that my beliefs about the nature of reality were too bizarre to share credibly as nonfiction. I guess I am over that, because I just shared a great deal of it with you. And I will be sharing a lot more before this book is done. If this highly imaginative and wildly speculative view of reality is something you are interested in, or compelled by, you have come to the right place.

It's time to get to the experience that I want to tell you about. It was an experience of what I later discovered is sometimes known as constant consciousness and it happened to me during the same long meditation retreat that I described earlier. I will preface this by saying that I was not a natural born meditator. The first time I tried to meditate I closed my eyes and sat quietly for what seemed like fifteen or twenty minutes. I opened my eyes to find that I had only been sitting for about three minutes. I concluded that meditation was a waste of time and vowed never to meditate again.

Things didn't turn out that way. After joining a spiritual community, I started meditating a minimum of one hour daily and doing multiple retreats a year. Unfortunately, every time I would meditate, I would fall asleep. No matter how awake I felt when I started, as soon as the bell rang, I would start nodding off. I tried for years to find a way to stay consistently awake through meditation, but nothing seemed to help. Sometimes it felt the harder I tried, the more I would sleep. When I began the retreat on which I experienced constant consciousness, I had decided first and foremost that I was not going to sleep - not once. We started meditating at 4:00am and did practice sessions until 10:00pm. Each hour I would sit wide awake. I would literally do anything to stay awake. I would tense my muscles. I would bite my tongue. I had vowed above all else to stay awake and I was committed to that.

After about three weeks on retreat there was one day when I felt particularly tired. By the time the last hour of meditation came at 9:00pm I was exhausted, and I was terrified that I would fall asleep. During that meditation I felt terrible. My eyes were burning, I had a headache, my muscles were sore all over. I was fighting to stay awake. I was almost hallucinating with exhaustion. It was very dramatic.

Finally, something unexpected happened. I heard a little voice in my head say to me, "You are not tired." That was it. Just a little statement that came to me in a soft voice. "You are not tired." For some reason that little statement triggered one of the most powerful spiritual openings that I've ever had. And it all started because when I heard that voice, I realized that it was true. I really wasn't tired. Sure, I was feeling the symptoms of a tired body. My eyes were burning, I had a headache, my muscles ached, but the part of me that was experiencing all those symptoms was wide awake. I was looking at the symptoms of a tired body, but the part of me that was looking was wide awake.

Suddenly in the middle of this sleepy hour, I was wide awake. But who was awake? A second ago I was sure that I was exhausted. Nothing had changed in my experience, yet suddenly I was wide awake. How was that possible? Who was tired a moment ago? Who is wide awake now?

During the rest of the hour of meditation I was simply sitting in shocked amazement. I was aware of the inside experience of my tired body, but it didn't feel like me anymore. It was my body, but I was only the awareness that was aware of the body. The body was tired, but I was not. I was wide awake and free. As I sat there feeling the difference between how my body felt, my true nature became more and more clear. I was not an organism that lived on the surface of a planet. I was a free-floating center of awareness that was emerging through the mind and body of an organism that lived on the surface of a planet. I was awareness. I was not a thing that was aware. I was awareness itself.

My body was just as exhausted as it had been a few minutes before, but it didn't bother me now. I realized that I was one hundred percent awake. I realized that I had always been one hundred percent awake and that I could never be anything less than one hundred percent awake. I was awareness. Awareness is always completely awake. It can't be turned off. It can't be less than completely awake, because it is awakeness itself. Awareness is always fully aware, and I am that. It was so obvious now that I had been identified with the experience of my body. I had thought that my body was me, so when my body was tired, I mistakenly thought that I was tired. No matter how tired my body got, the awareness that was aware of the experience of a tired body was always completely awake. It might be staring at the inside of a tired body, but it was still completely awake.

Imagine having your eyes open in a pitch black room. Your eyes are just as open to sight as they are on a bright day, it's just that there is nothing to see. Your eyes see equally well in the dark as they do in the light, they see mostly darkness at night because darkness is all there is to see. In the same way awareness is just as aware of a tired body as it is of morning sunshine upon waking. When the body is tired, that's what awareness is aware of. If awareness identifies with the body then it will assume that it is tired, but it is not, it is aware of tiredness, but it is always completely awake. I had never had a meditation like that before. Sitting there quietly was blissful joy. I never had to think about being tired or sleepy because I had forgotten how.

At some point the bell rang signaling the end of the meditation. I slowly stood up and walked away from my cushion. I could feel my body moving. I could see how my thoughts were directing it to move. But none of it felt like me. I was still the awareness that was aware of it all happening. I wasn't moving. I wasn't thinking. I was just watching, thinking and moving as it happened. It all seemed to be happening by itself. It seemed to me that the mind and body that I had thought was me, was not. The mind and body were completely capable of knowing that meditation had ended, deciding to get up and then actually getting up and walking away. I was not doing any of it. The mind and body were doing it all. It was as if my former mind, body, and self were on autopilot, and I was just watching them operate from the inside out.

I had become dislodged from any identification with my mind and body. It was obvious to me that I was a free-floating source of awareness, flowing through a mind and body that had mistakenly assumed it was that mind and body. That awareness never was the mind and body. It had always been a free-floating awareness. It was not floating in space. It was simply everywhere at once. The awareness that I was, seemed to exist everywhere at once. It was not located in any particular place. It was an awareness embedded within the fabric of reality everywhere. This mysterious awareness was who I was.

After meditation, I walked back to my bedroom and got ready to go to sleep. I lay down for a little while, continuing to marvel at everything that I was seeing. I watched as my body slowed down. I saw how my muscles relaxed and my breathing got quiet. I was aware of it all, but I wasn't doing any of it. It was all happening by itself. Eventually my body became very still and relaxed, and I felt a tingling sense of numbness in my toes. The tingling slowly moved through my feet and up my legs. It became stronger as it passed across my torso, shoulders, and arms. Then the tingling sensation engulfed my face and skull. I could hear a low hum as it passed my ears. My entire body was surrounded by a cloud of energetic numbness, and I could not move my arms or legs. Suddenly I realized I had fallen asleep!

I had fallen asleep, but I had not lost consciousness. I was still wide awake, but now I was wide awake to the inside of a sleeping mind and body. I continued to watch as my mind and body fell more deeply into sleep. My breathing became more and more automatic and regular. I started losing sensation in my limbs. My mind got very quiet. Soon I was floating in empty black space. I had no more body, and no thoughts, feelings, or sensations either. I knew nothing, I perceived nothing, I felt nothing, but I was somehow still present, blissfully floating in emptiness. I realized that both my mind and body had fallen completely to sleep, yet I was still there. I was not my mind or my body. I was the awareness that was aware of them.

But where was I? I could only imagine that I was in an empty space. But where was that space and what kind of space was it? There was nothing anywhere. There was nothing. As I rested in the deep peace of this empty space, I realized that this is where I always was. Even though I had been convinced throughout my whole life that I was a mind and body, the truth was I had always been the awareness that entered the mind and body from another dimension altogether.

As I floated freely as pure awareness, insights were being generated that appeared to illuminate my true nature. Somewhere beyond my familiar reality I have always existed as a source of pure awareness. Because I had dis-identified with my mind and body and they were now asleep, I returned to my true source. This is where I went every night while I slept. I was not unconscious; I was pure awareness with nothing to be aware of. This was how I was. This free-floating awareness that existed beyond the limits of time and space was my true self.

Suddenly a scene burst into existence. It was as if someone had turned a light on in the darkness. I found myself floating above the roof of a gas station and when I looked down, I saw myself lying on my back on the pavement. Then I snapped into my body, and I was looking up from the ground. I was dreaming. It was clear to me that my mind had snapped back on and had created this fictitious scene and placed me in it. It was all so real. The feeling of the pavement, the smell of gasoline in the air. It was perfectly real. And I was not alone. I was surrounded by twelve beautiful half-naked men. Their skin was dark, and they were naked from the waist up. Each of my arms and legs was being held by one of them. And they would periodically pull hard on my limbs as if they were trying to tear me apart. Those that were not pulling on my limbs were chanting something in unison. "You have to, you have to die" they said repeatedly.

As the drama of this little dream unfolded, I had the fascinating experience of having the perception of my dream-self laying on the ground being pulled apart, and as a free-floating perception from overhead. I was both in the dream and an observer of the dream watching it unfold. The part of me that was in the dream was only aware of the men standing around me and the pain I felt each time my limbs were pulled apart. That part of me was unaware of any other part of me, but the part of me that was watching the whole scene from someplace above, was simultaneously aware of being my dream-self as well. From above I marveled at how realistic the scene felt. It felt like reality, it didn't feel like a dream. And I could see how this scene was a perfect metaphor for the reality that I was discovering through the experience of constant consciousness. I was discovering that my normal personality only experienced its own perspective, but once I had dislodged from that identity, I experienced the free-floating nature of my true self. My true self seemed to be aware of both, the mind/body view of my personality, and the other worldly vantage point from another dimension.

This experience led me to conclude that my true essence was that of a free-floating pure awareness that existed in a dimension beyond time and space and only passed through the mind and body. For the next three days the experience of constant consciousness continued. I found myself walking around all day with part of my awareness looking out at the world from inside my mind and body, while my true self was a pure awareness, aware of everything from beyond time and space. It was as if I was in my mind and body and floating above them at the same time. It was clear to me that the free-floating pure awareness was my true, or at least truer, self and as the days of constant consciousness unfolded, I made a truly remarkable discovery. This free-floating awareness was who I was before I was born, and it is who I will be when my mind and body cease to function. I had discovered my eternal essence, my infinite soul, or something like that. My existential fear of death was gone. I had never been born and would never die. I am an eternal source of awareness that passes from lifetime to lifetime.

I realize that this was an interpretation of my experience, and you may think that the experience does not warrant such wildly speculative assertions. But from the point of view of having had this three-day experience, nothing was more obvious to me than what I just described. My true self is a pure awareness that exists in multiple dimensions of being. That awareness streams into this dimensional space through the personality of a mind/body system. The awareness that I am becomes mistakenly identified as the personality of the mind/body system. The spiritual path liberates the pure awareness from exclusive identification with the personality of the mind/body system so that it can recognize its own true nature. This pure awareness is who I was before this lifetime began and it is who I will continue to be when this lifetime comes to an end. I have no doubt about this, but that doesn't mean that it's true.

During the three days of my constant consciousness experience I was tempted at one point to come to a very different conclusion. During the third day, I began to wonder if I was losing my mind. I thought that I might be having a psychological episode, or even a psychic break, and I was contemplating writing a note to the retreat organizers explaining the situation and asking if I could see a doctor. That night I fell asleep and lost consciousness. Perhaps my fear that I was going crazy had broken the spell. I woke up in the morning and I didn't remember anything that had happened during the hours that I had fallen asleep. I had simply lost consciousness. Initially I was relieved, but then I was sad that my glorious experience had come to an end.

I wonder what would have happened if I had gone through

with the impulse to write a note and see a doctor. Perhaps the doctor would have agreed with me, suggesting I was experiencing psychological issues. Perhaps they would have prescribed some drugs, or maybe I would have had psychotherapy. That could have been the end of my spiritual life and I would be a very different person today. But that is not what happened. I didn't write a note, I didn't see a doctor, I stuck with the interpretation that seemed most obvious to me even if it fell outside of what was acceptable in the dominant paradigm of my culture.

Let's take a moment to think about how to assess the validity of our speculations. If we use the example of the experience of constant consciousness that I just described, we see that aside from a psychological disorder, it is hard to find an interpretation that fits within the current scientific paradigm. According to our scientific beliefs, consciousness is a property that is produced by the brains and nervous systems of living organisms. Therefore, consciousness cannot be free floating because it cannot exist outside of its host. What happens then when someone like me experiences their awareness free floating outside of the mind and body, even during sleep? How can that be explained?

William James was a truly original thinker and an academic superstar. He was one of the early pioneers of psychology and a globally recognized philosopher. He was also the president of the American Society for Psychical Research. The ASPR studied the trance mediums, psychics, and other phenomena of spiritualism. James thought that the study of unexplainable experiences was crucial to the future evolution of humanity. He recognized that the truly expansive potentials of human consciousness are not found in our ordinary experiences, but they can be seen at the fringes of possibility, in phenomena that we can't explain. These bizarre occurrences already show us that our current understanding of reality isn't big enough to explain everything and needs to be reconsidered.

James was also aware that science, the main tool of exploration in our society, is too often dismissive of anything it cannot explain or understand. James felt that this was very unscientific. He created an alternative way of thinking and he called his philosophy Radical Empiricism. Empiricism is the philosophy that says all knowledge should be rooted in our sensual experience of reality. In other words, our understanding should be based on the facts of our actual experience. If it cannot be verified in our experience, we should not believe it. James' Radical Empiricism went one step further. James felt that we should not believe in the reality of anything that we cannot verify in our actual experience. So, he was an Empiricist. But James also believed that we should not dismiss anything that is actually experienced by anyone unless we can verify that it is false. We must take all human experience seriously even if we cannot understand or explain it. It is unscientific to ignore any part of human experience until we can determine that it is invalid. Empowered with this attitude James risked his professional career by studying the paranormal and the supernatural.

In our exploration we are going to assume James' position. None of our paranormal, mystical, or supernatural experiences should be offhandedly dismissed just because we don't understand them or can't explain them. We are going to take them seriously and we are going to learn to interpret them in ways that make sense to us. We are going to take responsibility for creating our own understanding of reality, in ways that allow us to embrace all our experience. We will not dismiss anything that we actually experience unless we are convinced that it is in some way mistaken.

As I have embraced this position myself, I have come to a deeper understanding of the truly co-creative nature of reality. We don't just live in an objective reality that exists separate from us. We live in a reality that is shaped by both the experiences we have and the way we interpret those experiences. Because I developed an interpretation of my experience of constant consciousness that led to the conclusion that my true self was a free-floating source of awareness that existed in another dimension of reality, I began to experience myself this way more and more. In meditation I would often feel myself floating away from my body, even while I continued to feel solidly embedded in it at the same time. When we have the courage to embrace a paradigm breaking interpretation of our experience, we will create a momentum of understanding that tends to confirm that interpretation in our future experiences.

This is a point that I want to spend some time exploring with you. Our interpretations and conclusions about our spiritual experiences create the ground for the experiences and interpretations that we will have in the future. It might be helpful if we imagine reality as a field of possibility. Every moment potentially opens into an unknown number of possibilities. Which future possibilities actually open for us are determined, at least partially, by our current understanding of reality.

I want to suggest that a different model of reality will be helpful here. As we have already stated many times, we are trained to imagine that we live in a three-dimensional expanse of empty space filled with things. This is not a fact. I repeat, this is not a fact. This is the interpretation of reality that has been developed in the modern paradigm of scientific materialism. It is not a fact. We are taught that this interpretation is the one true fact about reality, and that any other interpretation must therefore be wrong. But this is not the case. This interpretation of reality is very useful in many ways, but that does not make it an indisputable fact. We experience the world around us as a three-dimensional expanse of space filled with things, but that is largely because we have been trained to experience it that way. We assume that because our experience so obviously and consistently demonstrates that we live in three dimensions of space filled with things, that it must be true. Please remember, that for hundreds of years people's experience told them the Earth was flat and that the Sun orbited around it. Neither was true.

Let's return to James' vision of a reality created entirely from instances of pure experience. Rather than a three-dimensional expanse of space filled with things we imagine reality to be a succession of moments of pure experience. Each moment of pure experience includes four elements. A background field of awareness, a foreground object of awareness, some relationship or attitude toward the object, and a sense of being the observer of the moment. This fourfold drop of pure experience is the only reality we will ever know and if we pay attention to our experience, we will find that we live through a never-ending succession of these drops of pure experiences. One after another after another.

It would be easy for us to relate to the image of a world of pure experience as something we live through. In other words, to imagine that we, the human being, live through a never-ending succession of moments of experience. But that is not what James meant. For James, there is no person having an experience of the moment. There is just an experience that includes an experience of being a person having the experience. There is no actual person that exists outside of the experience of the moment. We are not a person who is living through successive moments of experience. There is just a succession of moments of experience that include the experience of being a person living through them. There is no person, there is no person, there is no person. This is the hard part to get. Yes, intellectually it is not hard to understand the concept, but emotionally it is very hard to embrace it as true, or even possibly true.

Earlier I asked you to imagine that we are each dreaming our own reality into existence, but it is more accurate to think about a dream that dreams itself, without a separate person dreaming it. This is how I see reality. It is a dream that continually dreams itself into existence. The person that we are, the one that was born on our birthday here on Earth, is a character in the dream, a dream-self. The dream-self has a perspective from inside the dream and for many of us that is the only perspective we will ever know. We will live our entire lives and die in the dream of a three-dimensional universe. But some of us wake up to the possibility of a reality of pure experience. In that reality we are a dream-self, but we are also the dreamer of the dream, and we are the dream itself. There is no separate us that is having the dream or living through the dream. There is just a dream of existence, dreaming itself into being moment by moment by moment. There is no person or entity having the dream and there is no person or entity living through the moments.

And yet, as the dream-self we seem to have some degree of control over what we do in the dream. And one of the greatest powers we have is the power to creatively interpret our experience and draw new conclusions about the nature of reality. What I have discovered is that how we interpret reality and which conclusions we draw about the nature of reality have a profound impact in determining what can possibly appear in the next moment. Think about it. If I had interpreted my experience of constant consciousness as some form of mental aberration, then that would have opened to a certain set of possible next moments. Because I interpreted it as a revelation of my true nature as a free-floating pure awareness, it opened into a succession of ever deepening spiritual experiences that continued to expand and reinforce what I had experienced.

The way we interpret the experience of the current moment creates attitudes and filters that allow only certain next moments to appear. Different interpretations allow for different possible next moments. It is not that we are entirely creating reality as we go along, but we are guiding ourselves through an infinite sea of possible drops of pure experience. How those drops of pure experience unfold becomes our life. If we live inside an assumption of being an organism living in a preexisting three-dimensional reality, that assumption becomes the outer limit of what is possible. Discovering myself to be a free-floating source of awareness from another dimension opened a dramatic array of new possibilities.

Imagine that the drops of experience that arise as reality are all being fed from a vast multi-dimensional pluralverse. We have no way of knowing what possible shapes reality can take in any given instant of pure experience, but how the next instant actually appears for us is determined, at least in part, by how we interpret the current moment and what conclusions we draw from it.

This is a dramatically different way to envision reality. In theory it is not difficult to comprehend, but emotionally it is hard to embrace. Sit down right now and work with this vision. Look and see for yourself if reality is a moment of experience that includes a background field of perception, a foreground object of focus, an attitude toward the object, and a sense of being the observer of the moment. Could that drop of pure experience be the only reality? The interpretations and conclusions you come to in relation to this moment will determine what moment will open for you next. We live in a sea of infinite potential and how each next moment emerges out of that sea of potential is determined by our interpretations and conclusions of the current moment.

I realize that throughout this book I will be presenting different ways that I have come to see reality and they are not always congruent with each other. Some of the things that I believe and feel utterly convinced of, will be conflicting and maybe even mutually exclusive. This might bother you. You might feel that what I am saying cannot be true because it is self-contradictory. This would be a very valid concern if we lived in a universe that only contained one true reality because a single reality demands internal consistency. I believe that we live in a pluralverse in which many things that are real can be simultaneously true and conflicting. There might be a part of you that complains that I can't just make up the idea that we live in a pluralverse. I would counter by asking, "Why not? We made up the idea that we live in a universe and we seem happy enough with that." Hearing that comment you might demand that I provide proof. I would counter by demanding proof that we live in a universe.

We naturally feel a complaint when we are presented with theories that seem wildly speculative. Over the past eight hundred years in Western history, we have developed an allergic reaction to wild speculation. This conservative attitude in philosophy is often traced to the fourteenth century philosopher and theologian William of Ockham and the notion that came to be known as Ockam's razor. The idea can be simply stated as such; Given two theories that explain something equally well, the one that demands the least amount of speculation is always preferable. This seems sound enough. We currently explain how water boils in terms of energy being transferred into the molecules of the water. If we were presented with an alternative theory that claimed the reason water boiled was because tiny invisible starfish in the water were rubbing their arms together, we would see this as prosperous. It would seem ridiculous to speculate this wildly. What gives us any reason to believe in the existence of tiny invisible starfish, and how could we possibly know that rubbing their arms together caused water to boil. In a case like this, Ockam's razor seems very sound.

If we look more carefully, we will begin to realize that a lot of our current ideas, including ideas about atoms and molecules are also speculative and pretty wildly so at that. Because these ideas are familiar to us and because they have served us so well, we think of them as facts, but are they really? We have no idea what science will look like in the future, or which of our current beliefs will prove false. As an example, the famous Danish physicist Niels Bohr had a theory of the atom that most scientists, including Albert Einstein, believed must be true, for decades. That theory eventually proved false. The list of theories about reality that have proven false is much longer than the list that we still recognize to be true. And if you think about it, every scientific theory besides the ones we currently believe in, have proven false. Why would we think our current ideas about what is real will last forever?

It is good to have some humility when dismissing any well thought through theory about truth, but it might be crucial to our future that we increase our capacity to let go of even the longest lasting ideas of what is true. We live with a consistent sense that we more or less know what is real, and how reality works. Of course we know that we don't know everything, but still, we feel pretty confident in our fundamental understanding of reality. If it is true that our current understanding of reality is fairly close to what is actually true, as we tend to assume, then adhering to Ockam's razor is a good idea. Why introduce wild speculation into an understanding of reality that is fairly accurate already. On the other hand, if our current understanding of reality is far from accurate then wild speculation becomes more advisable.

Many people look at the state of our world and the various seemingly insurmountable global challenges we face as evidence that our understanding of reality and how reality works must be wildly off. If this is true, then being conservative in our speculations may be detrimental to the survival of our species and maybe even our planet. It is likely that we need to engage in wild speculation if we are going to find an understanding of reality that allows us to effectively deal with the challenges our world faces. This is a position that I first heard from the philosopher Timothy Morton of Rice University. Morton explained to me in a phone conversation that Western society has developed cultural antibodies to any idea that seems weird and if we are going to solve problems like global warming, we are going to have to find ways to think beyond those cultural inhibitors.

I experienced constant consciousness for three days. In that experience I recognized that I was not a conscious organism. I was a free-floating awareness from another dimension that was currently identified with a conscious organism. I cannot prove that this is true in any sense that would satisfy scientists of the current paradigm, but I have no doubt about it. It is the explanation that best fits the reality of what I experienced. And since then, that conclusion has been confirmed over and over again by many subsequent experiences. I believe that my willingness to embrace an alternative view of myself and reality has allowed a new reality stream to emerge in the sea of infinite possibility. I am living that stream and I am creating it at the same time. I am not trying to tell you that I am correct in my conclusions. I am inviting you to imagine doing the same for yourself and speculating about how your life might be different if you did.

You can also think of it like this, we all hold fundamental beliefs about who we are and how the world works. These rock-bottom beliefs about reality contain certain potentials. If I believe that I am an organic being whose conscious awareness is being produced by my brain and nervous system, then there are only certain possibilities that can unfold from there. Our foundational understanding of reality defines the sphere of possibility available to us. If we want to change the size and scope of the possibility field available to us, we must change our rock bottom beliefs.

CHAPTER FIVE

Kundalini Awakening

"There is no end to mystery."

- Anaïs Nin

Jeff Carreira

IN THE LAST CHAPTER I wrote about an experience of constant consciousness and how it set the stage for all the experiences I would have later, but it is also true that that experience was shaped by experiences I had had previously. For instance, I've talked about the dramatic emotional release that I experienced and what I had concluded about reality from that. That experience happened a decade earlier and those conclusions had been deeply incorporated into my fundamental understanding of reality by the time I experienced constant consciousness. In this chapter I want to explore an experience that I had only a few days before the experience of constant consciousness, which matches perfectly with what Eastern spiritual traditions describe as kundalini awakening. Both the constant consciousness and the kundalini awakening occurred during the same retreat and I want to say a little more about the context for that retreat, because it was the single most potent spiritual event of my life.

For twenty years I lived in a spiritual community, founded and led by a spiritual teacher who was always surrounded by controversy. The purpose of this book is not to critique the community, the teacher, or the teacher's methods. I can only say that for myself, I benefited immeasurably from my time there, and I feel that I learned as much from the teacher's shortcomings as I did from his strengths. One of the things that he was notorious for, and one of the things that attracted me to work with him in the first place, was his no-holds-barred attitude when working with students. The retreat that I was on when I experienced constant consciousness and kundalini awakening was a good example of that attitude in action. His methods were uncompromising, at times harsh, and sometimes arguably abusive. As I have become a teacher myself, I have tried to discover how to create an environment for spiritual growth that is both demanding and supportive. An environment that is always loving, even when clarity and strength is needed.

The preparation for the retreat I was on took place over nearly a year and included a relentless daily barrage of what is often called crazy wisdom. Crazy wisdom is an expression that refers to spiritual teaching methods that look insane when viewed in the light of conventional norms, but which are actually designed to be deeply psycho-spiritually liberating and activating. In terms of my teacher's methods, it remains unclear to me how much of it was authentic crazy wisdom and how much was just crazy. However, I cannot deny the life transforming power of what I experienced.

During the year leading up to that retreat my teacher worked intensively with a group of his students in extreme and sometimes bizarre ways. Once, I stood for the most part of a weekend outside in the freezing cold during a snowstorm, I attended hundreds of meetings designed to breakdown my resistances, I fell into a state of despair deeper than I had ever known before or since, I was wrestled into submission by three men to prove that I was willing to fight for my freedom, and in the end I was told to join a retreat with eleven other people.

The context for the retreat was stated clearly. It was to be a silent meditation retreat. We did not have to join, but if we chose not to, we were told that we would have to leave the spiritual community and break all contact with everyone in it. For me that meant losing the home that I had known for the past eight years, and contact with pretty much everyone I was close to. An additional catch was that we didn't know how long the retreat would last. We were told that "something" important needed to happen and that when it happened the retreat would end. That something was a very vague and elusive goal that we referred to as collective awakening. I was so intent on doing this retreat that I quit my job and gave up my career as a school teacher in order to be free to attend the retreat for as long as it lasted.

As the retreat started I was absolutely resolved to give every ounce of my energy and attention to it. In that context, I vowed that I would not doze off even once during the retreat and that commitment set the stage for the experience of constant consciousness that I described in the last chapter. But that experience was preceded by another dramatic experience that happened late one night about three weeks into the retreat. I woke up with a pain at the base of my spine. My tailbone felt as if it had been hit by a hammer. The pain was not imaginary. It hurt so badly that I got out of bed and started walking around my bedroom rubbing my tailbone. I couldn't imagine how I could have hurt myself. Maybe it was from the many hours of sitting in meditation. Could I have broken the tip of my tailbone from sitting so long? I didn't know what to do to make the pain go away. I was feeling desperate and wondered if I would need to leave the retreat to go to a hospital.

After a few minutes of walking around my bed and rubbing my tailbone, I realized the pain was not diminishing at all and out of frustration and exhaustion, I sat down on the edge of the bed. As soon as my tailbone hit the bed something happened. There was an inner explosion at the exact place that had been hurting so badly. It was an explosion of light and sound, and it immediately shot straight upward through my spine and out the top of my head. The blinding white light rushed through the top of my head with the pressure of a fire hose. As the light rushed through my head it roared with the sound of a lion. The light was hurting my eyes and the roar drowned out all other sound. My eyes were open at the time and I thought the light was in the room, so I closed them, but the light was on the inside too. The light roared through me for about thirty seconds and then all of a sudden it stopped. It was over and as the last of the roaring white hot light passed through me I felt no more pain. My body was exhausted as if I had just had a hard workout, my mind was empty and relaxed.

"I think that was kundalini!" I said aloud to myself. I had read about kundalini, but not extensively. The awakening of kundalini was not an explicit part of the spiritual path that I was on, but of course it is a big part of the Hindu tradition so I did know something about it. This experience undoubtedly matched many of the descriptions that I had read about kundalini and I felt confidence that that's what it was. Later, after the retreat had ended, I spoke to my teacher about the experience. He told me that he had had an almost identical experience early on in his spiritual search. I was very excited about this experience for a few days and we had a number of discussions about it. Eventually he got annoyed with me for bringing it up yet again and he asked me sarcastically, "So, what do you think you're enlightened now?" It was clear from his tone that I wasn't, and I never brought it up with him again.

The spiritual path that I was on was based on my teacher's interpretation of the Hindu tradition of Advaita Vedanta. To him the whole purpose of spiritual pursuit was total inner freedom. That meant freedom from needing or even preferencing anything to be different than it already was. It meant being totally content with exactly the way things are, without any need for more. In this context spiritual experiences were encouraged and honored, but only to a certain extent. Journey's into alternative realities were also seen as potential distractions from the larger goal of total inner freedom. If we become overly fascinated with breakthrough experiences like the ones that I describe in this book, we might lose interest in the holy grail of liberation and emancipation. My teacher would sometimes say that you could spend five minutes relishing in the glory of a dramatic opening and then you had to let it go and move on.

There is a great deal of wisdom in this point of view, although later I wondered to what extent my teacher's position was influenced by his own personal desire to be the only enlightened one in the community. I suspect that a selfish motive was alive in him, but I can honestly say that my own growth was served well by maintaining this attitude. I believe that my willingness to let go of the experience of constant consciousness I described earlier was crucial to my continued spiritual growth. I have met so many people who spent decades of their spiritual path trying to recreate an experience they once had. Most often that is a fruitless effort. And even in those rare occurrences where the original experience is recreated, it seldom leads to the transformation imagined. My experience tells me that it is best to embody the experiences we have fully, let them affect us, change us, and then move on to whatever's next. We will explore more about why this is the case in the last chapter, but right now I want to share a little about how my initial interpretation of the kundalini experience has changed over time.

Because of the spiritual path I was on, I had also consciously attempted not to make too much out of my experience of kundalini awakening. I reminded myself that any experience, no matter how powerful or glorious, was only an experience and needed to be let go of. I went back to my practice without attempting to reignite that energy or dwell on it in any way. I simply sat in meditation and let everything be as it is. I can't say that I forgot about it, but I really didn't hold on to it at all.

An interesting epilogue to the story is that ten years later when my spiritual community disbanded, the first thing I started thinking about was that kundalini experience. I realized that I had always wondered if I had missed something in that experience. Some years earlier, I had been in contact with a kundalini teacher named Dorothy Walters, and I decided to ask her about it. I told her that I wanted to explore the path of kundalini and described my previous experience. When I was done with my description she said, "I don't know why you want to pursue more kundalini experience, you've already had the experience that everyone is hoping for." That simple statement was deeply affirming. We continued to talk for about an hour as she asked me questions about my kundalini experience and everything that happened in my spiritual life after that.

As we spoke, Dorothy re-contextualized my spiritual life until I began to see that everything that happened to me spiritually after that kundalini experience could be seen as the result of how that energy was making its way through my being and unraveling the karma that bound me. Dorothy took every next experience I described in my spiritual history during and after that retreat and wove it into a tapestry of ever-expanding kundalini awakening. It was thrilling to see my own most intimate story rewritten before my very eyes. I was thrilled to get a new perspective on my life - not because I thought it was more true than what I already believed, but because I knew that it was another dimension of the truth. It was not replacing what I knew, it was adding to it. I was seeing more of what was already there. I was seeing more of myself and more of my journey. This conversation led me to a new desire to explore energy work, not because I felt like something was missing, but because I now saw that there was a whole new perspective on my experience that I could explore.

Initially I interpreted the kundalini opening as fascinating, but not significant. In fact, I eventually came to believe that giving it too much attention was a distraction from the real goal of spiritual freedom. Because that is the way I interpreted the experience, I didn't pursue it and therefore I didn't have more energetic openings, or, if I did, I didn't recognize them as such. That was the point that we ended the last chapter with. We live in a universe of unfolding possibility. How we make meaning out of our experience of life determines what possibilities open for us to step into and which remain hidden. Now that Dorothy had opened the door to an energetic interpretation of spiritual life, I felt compelled to explore it.

The first energetic work that I explored after my spiritual community disbanded was kundalini yoga. I found a teacher who offered two practice sessions every week in Philadelphia where I lived. I participated in these sessions for about six months. We did breathing exercises with physical movements. I would always feel energy rising up from the floor through my body and occasionally I would feel the energy very strongly and it would last for hours after the session. It also seemed to me that my access to the energy was becoming more consistent and deeper.

Eventually my kundalini yoga teacher needed to take a break from teaching because she was pregnant, and before I had found another teacher to work with, something unexpected took me in a different direction. I happened to be going to visit friends in Hawaii, and before I left, another friend told me about a massage therapist I should see while I was there. Her name was Jody Mountain and I was told that she was very special. Jody was giving massages in a very typical massage studio on Maui. Given the recommendation I had received I was expecting something special, but I had no way of knowing what was about to happen.

Jody's massage was a life-transforming event, subtle but profound. It is hard to describe exactly what happened. I walked in and lay down on the table. In many ways the massage was ordinary enough, except that I felt like I was outside of my mind from the start. The best way I can describe it, is to say that Jody's body and my body were having a conversation that neither of our minds were involved in. I felt as if there was an energy that was connecting us and that energy was guiding the massage. It felt deeply intimate, but not personal, because my personality wasn't part of it. When it was over I was stunned by the experience. I asked Jody what kind of massage it was and slowly she began to tell me that she was an adept at an indigenous Hawaiian form of massage known as Ancient Lomi Lomi.

A few weeks later I was home on a very hot day sitting by the side of another friend's pool. I was thinking about the massage and I was reading blog posts that Jody had written. As I read each post an intense energetic vibration would over take my body and I would heat up until I was sweating profusely. Eventually I would dive into the pool to cool off then climb back up and start reading another. Over and over again, I experienced these surges of energy that forced me into the pool to cool off. I had no idea what was happening, but my connection with Lomi Lomi was obviously creating a huge energy opening in me. I registered for Jody's next ten day retreat that same day and a few months later I was in Hawaii learning how to give Ancient Lomi Lomi massage ceremonies. That retreat was amazing and I was hooked. Over the next two years, despite an already over-packed schedule, I managed to give nearly two hundred massage ceremonies.

Lomi Lomi opened me up to the life force energy of Mana and as I explored this massage form I was thrilled to discover that I could intuit my way through a massage rather than thinking my way through it. In Jody's retreat we were trained to not think about what we were doing, but rather to feel our way through it. I was trained to put my attention on the experience of contact between my skin and the skin of the person I was working on. The sensation of contact contained all of the information I needed to follow. My mind's ideas were not useful. At the beginning it felt like operating in the dark, because I was so used to navigating life through the models and concepts I held in my mind. Eventually I found that I could follow my body's intelligent wisdom and navigate through the massage in a flowing and spontaneous way. I found profound congruence with the meditation practice that I taught. In meditation, I teach people to let go of all their ideas about the practice, or how to do it, or what the goal is, and then simply follow the direction that the present moment invites them into.

Lomi Lomi opened me to a new domain of intelligence, the wisdom of the body. We are trained to think of thoughts as containing wisdom, but feelings less so. Now I was seeing that feelings and physical sensations contain wisdom and intelligence that can be an invaluable guide through life.

I had so many powerful experiences while giving massages and each one opened me a little more. I eventually did a second ten-day retreat with Jody, and both of my retreat experiences with her were profound. It is beyond the scope of this book to describe much more about Lomi Lomi and what it means to me, but I know without doubt that it changed my life.

I see a very direct line leading from my conversation with Dorothy Walters about my kundalini awakening, to my work with kundalini yoga, and finally to my discovery of Ancient Lomi Lomi. This is a perfect example of the point I am making in this book. I had the experience of kundalini awakening about twelve years before I would speak with Dorothy about it. During those twelve years I had many spiritual experiences and breakthroughs, but none of them appeared to me to be directly connected to the kundalini experience. After speaking with Dorothy, I began to see how the energy of kundalini had played a part in all of my subsequent experiences, and more importantly I found myself consciously on a path of energetic awakening.

Speaking with Dorothy radically altered my interpretation of my kundalini experience. I had previously recognized it as amazing, but ultimately concluded that it was not very significant and potentially a distraction from the real path. With that interpretation in place there was very little room to pursue the experience further, and I didn't tend to see any of the experiences I would go on to have, as connected to it. Once Dorothy convinced me to take the experience seriously, I started to see evidence of it everywhere, and even more importantly, opportunities began to open up for me. This is the point I have been making throughout this book, - how we interpret and make meaning of our spiritual experiences affects what possibilities open up for us. Dorothy helped me see new meaning and significance in my kundalini awakening and that opened up a new range of possibilities that led me to the work of Lomi Lomi, a form of energetic work that introduced significant changes in my life.

I've already said that the two month retreat during which I experienced constant consciousness and kundalini awakening, was the most transformative event of my life. I had dozens of other spiritual openings during that retreat, including an experience of cosmic awareness that I will describe in the next chapter. Perhaps, the single most transformative experience I had on that retreat was a collective awakening, which is another experience that today, I see differently as a result of the conversation I had with Dorothy.

The experience of collective awakening was the true holy grail of my spiritual community and the path I pursued whole-heartedly for two decades. In fact, all of the practice and study we did, as well as the inner freedom we won as a result, were seen as being in service of our shared quest for collective awakening. My teacher had realized early in his teaching career that when inspired and awakened people come together, a field of awakened consciousness is generated between them. As a community our mission was to ignite and stabilize between us, a shared state of awakened awareness. We believed it would be possible to generate a living field of consciousness between us, that would become, in a sense, awake independently from us. It would be something like a culture. The people who live within a culture share certain views and perspectives, but people can come and go and the cultural view remains. We believed that something similar could happen with an awakened culture. We were determined to ignite a field of awakening that would stabilize between us and remain in existence even as individual members came and went. We were determined to liberate awakening itself from its attachment to any individuals. In doing this, a field of awakening would be born, that was held by a group of people, but not dependent on any one of them.

Collective awakening was the context for the retreat I was on. The goal of the retreat was to catalyze an experience of collective awakening among the participants. None of us were exactly sure what that would look like, but our teacher assured us that he would know when it had happened, and that is when the retreat would end. After everything we had gone through leading up to the retreat and then giving up my career to be on it, I was not going to waste a single moment. I started, determined to give every ounce of my energy to the spiritual practice I would be doing. I was determined that we would give birth to a field of collective awakening. And about six weeks into the retreat we did experience a profound and dramatic collective awakening.

In truth, the collective awakening actually started with some people who were not on retreat. We later heard that this group had started meeting outside of the retreat and some of them had begun to speak from a source that was distinctly different. They spoke with a depth of spiritual clarity and conviction that was undeniably profound to those around them. At some point those of us on the retreat were told that we would be meeting nightly together with these people from outside the retreat.

Meetings of this type were always a big part of our community life, so much so in fact that we would jokingly say, "I meet therefore I am." We all believed that it would be in a meeting like this that the elusive goal of collective awakening would emerge. So when we started meeting on the retreat and we were told that something amazing had already started to happen, I was both thrilled and a little scared. I remember the first meeting. The twelve of us on retreat were sitting in a circle along with eight others who were not on the retreat. Some of the people who were joining from outside the retreat were obviously speaking from a different place. They spoke with an intensity of deep knowing that felt intimidating. We had all been in hundreds of meetings by then and had heard many people speaking in profound ways, but this was different because it wasn't forced in any way. It was as if those who were speaking with such depth were simply speaking and explaining what they now saw so plainly right in front of them. I could see in their eyes that they were looking at something and describing it to me. They were not sharing ideas, they were describing a reality that they were seeing.

They were in this world physically, but they were seeing another world entirely. Their eyes revealed that they were not all here, they were at least half in some other dimension. The most exciting thing was that it was not just one person in that state, there were three or four who seemed to be in the higher state together. It was obvious hearing them speak that they were inhabiting the same new world of higher illumination. They spoke of subtle truths, not from memory, but from direct seeing. They were describing the invisible workings of the spiritual world because they were seeing it at work - and they were all seeing the same world.

The goal of our meetings were for all of us, about eighteen by then, to join the first few in that other world. We met night after night and I tried to join in that higher state by doing the only thing that I could think to do, mimic what I saw in them. I was trying to fake it. Each time I tried my words landed flat. It was clear to everyone that I was not abiding in the higher place. I could even recognize it in myself. I could see that they were all in a different world of perception, but I didn't know how to enter it with them. Eventually someone else in the circle stepped across that invisible threshold into another dimension. As this new inhabitant spoke, you could see something different in their eyes. They were wide with wonder. Their inner gaze was moving from place to place in amazement. Their words rang true with the quiet confidence of direct seeing. They were in. Once the first person stepped across, another soon followed. After a few nights there were only a few of us left who were still yet to make that leap. I was one of the remaining few.

One night I found myself in complete despair. I had tried every way I could think of to step into the clarity of direct seeing with my spiritual compatriots, but nothing worked. I felt like I would never be able to see what they were seeing - to be where they seemed to be. Then, without realizing it, I did the one thing that I had not tried before. I gave up. I quit. It was too much for me. I was never going to be able to do it. I remember looking down at the ground in full acceptance of my utter inadequacy to the task at hand. And as I looked down, something happened.

Energy started to move through my body and up and out through the top of my head. I felt as if I could see the stars of an infinite cosmos through a gaping hole in my skull. Inwardly I became very still and calm and I started feeling something stirring in my chest. Something wanted to be spoken, but it wasn't me. It was pushing to come out of me. I felt fear, but I was not afraid. It was as if there was some other being inside me that wanted to come out. I relaxed.

I felt my mouth open, I saw my fist slam down on the ground and these words came out of my mouth. "I am here!" That is all I said in that first burst. I am here. And it didn't feel like me, Jeff, talking. Someone else had arrived. In that moment of speaking Jeff and whoever had just spoken, revealed themselves to be one. I, the bigger I, had arrived. Suddenly everything was different. All of the words that I had heard the others speaking for over a week didn't sound like words. They were simply a description of what I was now seeing. They were not ideas, they were reality. I felt like I was seeing how it all worked. I saw how my body and personality were a vehicle for a source of life that was everywhere. I saw that I was that source even as I was an expression of it. It was clear that the idea of being Jeff had been speaking through the mouth on my face for my whole life, but now life itself was speaking through me instead. And that same source of life was speaking through every other person who had stepped across the threshold. When I saw one of them speak I knew it was life speaking through them and I knew I was that life.

I, Jeff, did not feel like I had awakened. I, Jeff, had stepped aside and life was awake and in control now. Life was thrilled to have access to so many of us at the same time. Where I had seen a conversation between individuals just a moment before, I now saw a higher mind thinking out loud to itself. A higher consciousness was able to interact with itself through us. It was the most thrilling communion I had ever experienced. As I sat through that meeting more and more wisdom came through me, but it was not coming from things that I already knew, it was a simple description of what was now being seen. The higher intelligence was using our group to explore itself. It was drawing on the experience of the individuals to articulate itself into greater manifestation. It was seeing itself, articulating itself, and bringing itself to life, between us. I was watching what we would later refer to as the birth of a Higher We.

A few more nights went by and there was only one person left who had not crossed the threshold. There was an enormous amount of pressure on them to let go and step through. We could all feel that something wanted to happen, but it needed everyone present to arrive. Eventually it happened. The last person finally relaxed all effort and allowed something else to speak through them. I don't remember what they said, but I remember that it was simple and quiet and humble. I remember that it was unmistakably from the higher source and it dramatically shifted the energy of the room. I saw a stream of energy that started to swirl faster and faster around our circle. It was passing through each of us accelerating as it did. The hole in the top of my head got wider and eventually I saw the swirling energy shooting out of my head and everyone else's up through the roof and into the sky. The roar was tremendous. I hadn't connected it at the time, but when I described this to Dorothy Walters later, she remarked that it sounded like a collective kundalini experience to her.

At the time, I hadn't thought so much about the energetic part of the experience, because I had been trained not to, but later I realized that it was an important part of what was happening. My interpretation of that event was about a higher being that was emerging through us, not about kundalini awakening in a group, but now I see that both interpretations fit, and both bring out different aspects of the experience and open up new potentials and possibilities.

Now that everyone had let go, it was clear that the goal we had been seeking had occurred. The energy of awakening was now independently alive. It was emerging through the individuals, but it had a life of its own. We remained on retreat for two more weeks, and each night we met in the rapture of collective realization. We saw how it all worked more clearly each night, but more importantly the higher being saw itself more clearly each night. During the day, those of us who were on retreat would sit in super charged silence. Every night we would meet in the ecstasy of realization. Perhaps the most amazing thing was that each night as the higher being came alive between us, it was not the same. It seemed to have grown and developed since the night before. It felt as if it were alive. We had given birth to something that was now alive and independent of us.

Eventually we were told that the emergence had happened and that the retreat was now over. My life changed radically after this. I became my teacher's personal assistant, a position I would hold for the next twelve years. I, and the other retreatants, started leading special discussion groups we called *enlightened communication discussions*. In them we found we could now consistently evoke some degree of that shared experience of awakening. I lead groups in cities across the United States, Canada, throughout Europe and in Australia. And in each group I experienced a kind of psychic liftoff into shared higher awareness. Perhaps not as strong as I had experienced on retreat, but strong enough to leave most people in awe and keep them coming back to join similar discussions regularly.

Before moving on to the next chapter, we need to consider the co-creative power of how this experience was interpreted, not just by me, but by everyone present. We were all already in a conversation about the birth of a Higher We, so when the emergence occurred between us, the language of the Higher We was what we naturally used to describe and understand what was happening. We interpreted the collective experience as a higher being, which we saw as a higher level of consciousness that existed beyond the sense of separation that we experience in our normal human form. As individuals rose up to that higher collective level of consciousness, we saw it as a new being that included all of us but also existed beyond us, and that is exactly how it felt.

On retreat, during the day, I would walk around feeling more or less normal. Of course I was profoundly energized by the excitement of discovery, and my meditation practice was amazing, but I still generally felt like Jeff. I felt like an individual completely and distinctly apart from the people around me. Of course, because of what I was experiencing every night, I knew this wasn't true, but it still often felt as if it was. Each night we would start our meeting by sitting quietly together. I would look down at the floor in front of me and relax. Slowly my head would open to the cosmos and the stars above. I could almost see the energy of the higher being, as it began to swirl faster and faster between us. Then it would enter someone and inhabit their body and words would start pouring out of their mouth. Sometimes it was me whom the energy would enter, and I would feel words flowing through my mouth. I didn't know what I was going to say. It was profoundly spontaneous and it felt like something was speaking through me. During those meetings, no matter whose eyes I looked into, I saw the higher being behind them. We were one being. Later, when Dorothy Walters described it as a shared kundalini awakening, I saw how the energy of kundalini had been working its way through each individual until it had free access to all of us. The swirling energy that moved through us was kundalini, the energy of awakening.

This intensity of unity did not last for long after the retreat ended, but it never entirely dissipated either. The sense of a higher being was now a permanent part of my experience. It always seemed to be there, and occasionally it would come forward. I remember once having a meeting about mundane matters and suddenly everyone flipped into the higher we consciousness. We worked out a complex and emotionally charged situation remarkably quickly and easily because in that unitive consciousness everyone wanted to come to a mutually recognized truth as quickly as possible. No one felt separate, so no one was championing their own point of view over the truth. Everyone just wanted to be open and vulnerable. We all felt that this kind of experience would change the world.

From one point of view you might wonder what difference it really makes whether you call the energy a higher being or kundalini, but it might matter a great deal. I know we had interpreted it as a higher being at the time, but I will never know what possibilities might have opened up if we had called it kundalini. What I do know is how my experience opened up once again, when I started to see the possible significance of spiritual energy and kundalini. I know that after that conversation with Dorothy I felt compelled toward energy work and eventually found Ancient Lomi Lomi. I know how much I feel my own growth and connection to divinity has been opened up by that exploration. There isn't space in this book to share all of the avenues of exploration that opened up for me as a result of my energetic explorations. I explored breathwork and dance practices. I met other practitioners and teachers who were adept in spiritual worlds that I had never been a part of. In my own teaching work

I began to leave space for energetic work. And because there was space for it, the energy of awakening started to show up more.

It was around this time of energetic exploration that I developed a friendship with Dr. Jeffrey Kripal. I feel that he and I have one of those magical friendships. I have read a great deal of his work and I so often feel that we are resonant frequencies. Not identical in tone, but perfectly complementary. One of the things that we have discussed is the importance of embracing both the cognitive and the energetic aspects of awakening. Jeffrey told me that he admired that I was willing to embrace both.

One aspect of awakening is the expansion of our consciousness. In this aspect, we become less reactive to the thoughts and feelings that arise in our minds. As a result we begin to see more of what was always there. Our attention expands beyond our previous perceptual habits and we see that we are much more than we had thought. We become sensitive to perceptual input that was simply beyond our capacity to sense before. We open to new dimensions of ourselves and the world. We begin to have insights and realizations that we could not have had before. We feel as if we are seeing the secret inner workings of everything. The other aspect of awakening is an energetic release and acceleration. We feel that the energy within us is being intensified and the frequency of vibration is dramatically increased. Jeffrey described it to me in a phone call we had, as an encounter with a higher energy that comes from another dimension of being or maybe even a higher dimensional being. That energy enters us, inhabits us and alters us so that we can accommodate at least some of that more intense higher vibrational energy in the world.

Both of these aspects of awakening need to be embraced. The expansion of consciousness is essential for us to enter new worlds of possibility and live there. At the same time, we need to be able to hold the higher energies of those new possibilities. Looking back on my spiritual life through the lens of this new energetic perspective reveals that higher energies were always a part of my breakthrough experiences, even if I was not paying attention to them. I can see that in some ways I was doing energetic work even if I didn't think about it that way. Perhaps there is no way to completely avoid working with both halves of the awakening process. I think that is because awakening must happen in both our minds and our bodies. The more cognitive practices like meditation and prayer emphasize the expansion of the consciousness, energetic practices like breathwork and yoga emphasize using the body to open higher energies of being. I was always someone who relied on my intellect, so perhaps it was natural for me to enter a spiritual path that emphasized the expansion of consciousness. All I needed was a different interpretation of my previous experience to open a new and exciting avenue of spiritual exploration. I feel that I am a more full and balanced human being as a result and I have a deep and profound respect for the energetic aspects of our being.

CHAPTER SIX

Cosmic Awareness

*"Truth is a pathless land, and you cannot approach it by
any path whatsoever, by any religion, by any sect."*

~ J. Krishnamurti.

IN THIS CHAPTER I WILL be describing another experience I had on that two-month retreat and use it to explore a mysterious vision of the full scope and scale of the spiritual life. The experience that I am about to describe happened in between the kundalini awakening and the collective awakening described in the last chapter. You will remember that part of the collective awakening experience for me involved my head seemingly opening to the cosmos. What you will see by the end of this chapter is how spiritual experiences build on one another. Each spiritual breakthrough creates the ground for the next. Each next breakthrough opens doors of possibility that were previously closed. My spiritual life has been punctuated by numerous breakthrough experiences and looking back on it I can see how each one opened and illuminated the path forward. They created a path to be followed, each one became another stepping stone along the way. Each one pushing past the edge of the possible to create a bridge to take me deeper into the unknown unknown beyond. The path of spiritual experience is like driving a train while you are laying down the tracks at the same time. There is no present path, the path emerges as each next breakthrough illuminates only the very next step.

From the very start of that long retreat my experience of meditation was deep and consistent. When I wasn't having powerful breakthroughs, I was just sitting and letting everything be as it was. Initially there was more of a sense of anxiety and desire for things to be different, but fairly quickly that faded and I became deeply content with whatever was happening. It was during one quiet day on retreat that something amazing happened. What I remember about that day is that it was just an easy day of meditation. The evening meetings that I described in the last chapter hadn't happened yet. All day long I just sat quietly. I was meditating with my eyes open, gazing lightly toward the floor in front of me. As I sat, I would get deeply relaxed. My eyes would slowly become unfocused until the floor in front of me was a blur. Thoughts, feelings, and sensations would come and go. Sometimes I would have realizations and insights. Sometimes not. No matter what happened, I just sat.

It was in one of these very peaceful meditations that I had the very disconcerting feeling that I was floating off the ground. By that point in the retreat so many extraordinary things had happened, including the kundalini experience I described in the last chapter, that I wasn't surprised by this. It was just one more unimaginable thing. I watched as my line of sight rose higher in the room. There are moments in our meditation practice that are crucial and extraordinary. They are moments when something unusual starts to happen. These anomalous events are part of what we want to have in our practice, yet in the moment when something truly unusual begins to happen we often recoil away from it. Part of the practice of meditation involves becoming untethered from the way things are. When we do, we become available to be moved, to be carried off into new vistas of reality. When that mysterious movement into another dimension of possibility begins it can be shocking and terrifying. If we have not established an unshakable capacity to relax and allow, we will recoil reflexively. We will stop whatever process has begun. Once we stop that mysterious journey, we can't simply restart it. Those moments come and go as they please. My experience has shown me that if you follow them, more will come, but if you pull back you will have to wait for another opening, if one comes at all. If you reject them, even unconsciously, you may be waiting a long time for another chance.

When I teach meditation to people who are looking for dramatic life-transforming experiences, I tell them that these extraordinary moments are what we are practicing for. We spend hours just sitting and learning to let everything be as it is. We build a tremendous capacity to be nonreactive and calm no matter what happens. We are practicing equanimity in part for those moments when the world moves under our feet, and we begin to feel ourselves carried away into spiritual realms and other dimensions. If we have built a powerful habit of non-reactivity, we will remain calm and allow something extraordinary to happen.

That is what I did the day I found myself floating up toward the ceiling. I was tempted to move my head and look to see if I was really floating, but I didn't. Just that little movement to check and see what was happening would have been enough to halt the process. A recoil doesn't have to be a huge contraction. Any way we attempt to compare the strange occurrence that has started, against the background of our ordinary perception, will shut it down. In this case the temptation was to look at the floor and my body to see if what I was experiencing was "real," by looking to see if my physical body had actually left the ground.

I just sat still with my eyes looking downward. The floor moved further and further away. My line of sight got closer and closer to the ceiling. I was certain I would bang my head, but I didn't. Instead, my head floated up through the ceiling. I saw into the rafters above as I passed through them. I remained calm and quiet as I floated up. My eyes passed through the roof, and I was outside, above the building. I could see the town all around me. At this point I no longer felt as if I was in my body. I didn't need to turn my head to see around me. I could see in all directions at once. I could see the church steeple on the other side of town. I could see the large lake beyond it. I floated up higher and higher and I could start to see over the nearby mountains to the city thirty miles away. I floated up, up, up. Eventually, I couldn't see any of the buildings in town clearly. I could see the light from cities a hundred miles away. Soon I had a vantage point that I had only enjoyed in airplanes. Soon I was up so high I could see the round shape of Earth. I expanded until Earth was just another dot of light. At this point I realized that I was not just floating upward, I was expanding in all directions. Eventually all the stars and galaxies of the cosmos were inside my body. There the expansion stopped.

The entire cosmos was my body. I was a universal being. I was the living universe in which my life on earth was a tiny part. At this moment I had the most wondrous sense of complete and utter relaxation. I felt like I had finally come home. I was being bathed in a sense of love and care that left me feeling completely open and receptive. Nothing could possibly hurt me because I was a being of love in an infinite sea of love. There was only care and concern and nothing else. I rested in that expansive state and absorbed all the love and care. Then I started to sink downward again. Back down toward the earth and then the town. Finally, I was sitting again on the floor gazing down at the pattern on the carpet.

It is not clear to me when, but at some point, I remembered that I used to expand into my true cosmic self when I was a young child. At about the age of three or four I would regularly lock myself in my parents' bathroom and stare into my eyes in the mirror. I would expand up through the ceiling and out into the furthest reaches of the cosmos, just like I did on retreat. I remembered the day I went into the bathroom, stared into the mirror, and couldn't do it anymore. I had forgotten how. I remember feeling crushed that I had lost my way home. Now I found my way again. I had found my way back to my true self. From this experience I knew that I was a cosmic being. I was the cosmos itself.

I believe that the entire cosmos, all of creation, is one singular living conscious and compassionate being. I believe this is what religious traditions are referring to when they use the word god. I am that being, and so are you, and so is everyone. The compassionate awareness of the cosmic being is passing through each of us right now. The awareness that is reading this book is coming from the being of the entire cosmos. It is not just you who is reading, the cosmos is reading through you. While I write this book, it is not just me writing it, the cosmos is writing it through me. There is one being in the cosmos, and we are all a manifestation of that. That is the conclusion I have come to. I cannot prove it. I can only tell you that my experience has convinced me it is true, even though the words I use to describe it will never give it justice. I am sure that the reality that I am trying to describe as a cosmic being is infinitely vast and more mysterious than any words could hold.

As I already mentioned, this experience of cosmic awareness happened between the kundalini experience and the constant consciousness experience. One of the things that I hope to illustrate with this book is how our spiritual experiences and the way we interpret them, creates our spiritual path. A different succession of breakthrough experiences will carve out a different path. And, as we have been saying, the same experiences interpreted in different ways will also carve out a different path. As I look back, I see that spiritual energy was established as part of my path when I had a kundalini awakening. Somehow that experience broke through an inner barrier that allowed me to experience the cosmic nature of my being and remember my early childhood knowledge of my true nature.

I also see how the experience of cosmic awareness set the stage for my next experience of constant consciousness by giving me a context for accepting the reality of it. If my awareness was ultimately coming from the living being of the cosmos, then certainly it didn't go off at night. There are billions of people living all over the surface of this planet and at least millions are awake at any given time. The cosmic awareness that shines through them must always be present. During the days that I experienced constant consciousness, it was clear to me that it was a source of awareness from beyond this world. I thought of it as the awareness of the cosmos. It felt as if I had slipped out of my individual awareness into the awareness of the cosmos.

It seemed very reasonable to wonder why I couldn't see through everyone's eyes. Since my awareness was emanating from the ever-present awareness of the cosmos, why was I only able to see through the eyes in this body? The awareness that was now constantly mine, was the same awareness that was passing through every eye of every being on the planet. I spent a few hours of meditation trying to see through everyone else's eyes. We were all sitting on the floor meditating for hours a day. During some of those hours I tried to let go of my individual perspective and relax so that I could see through everyone's eyes. I imagined that if I could do it, I would suddenly see twelve different perspectives in the room. I was never able to do it and I concluded that the habit of seeing through only one set of eyes was too strong for me to break.

This was my path, but it could have been different. I might have had other experiences, or the same experiences but interpreted them differently. I might have concluded that the energy of kundalini was the key to my awakening and become overly involved trying to generate more of it. Perhaps that would have meant that I never had the experience of cosmic awareness I just described. Instead the idea that kundalini was the awakening energy of the cosmos, seemed to set the stage for an opening to cosmic awareness, and that led to an opening of the ever-present consciousness of the cosmos pouring constantly through me. What if I had been on a Christian retreat and had identified the energy of kundalini as the love of God. What experience might that interpretation have led to? How might my retreat have unfolded differently?

At this point you might be wondering which interpretation of the experience is correct. Was it kundalini energy that rushed through my body? Or was it the love of God? I don't believe there is a correct interpretation. Or it might be better to say that many, perhaps every, interpretation could be correct. This is where we must relax into pluralism again. I believe that fluidity and freedom on the spiritual path necessitates that we embrace a reality where more than one thing can be true. To the ears of the modern paradigm this cannot make sense. Reality is defined as the way things are. Since there is only one reality, there can be only one truth about it. If we live under the assumption of there being only one truth, then we must be concerned with whether we have made the right interpretations and come to the right conclusions, and the right interpretations and conclusions of our experience is the one that reflects the actual reality behind the experience.

If we believe that there is a reality that exists beyond our perception of it, then there is only one correct way to interpret our experiences. An energetic awakening either is, or is not, an experience of kundalini energy. My experience of cosmic awareness either does, or does not, reveal that we are a cosmic being. Constant consciousness either is, or is not, a revelation of universal awareness. The same experience cannot both be a kundalini awakening and the love of God. Unless kundalini awakening and love of God are two phrases that signify the same thing. Then a rose by any other name smells as sweet. What if kundalini awakening is one thing, and the love of God is another? And, we can interpret our energetic experience either way? How do we choose between those two, or any number of other possible alternatives?

One who lives by William James' philosophy is called a radical empiricist. As I understand it, a radical empiricist recognizes that reality is pluralistic, that more than one thing can be true at the same time, even if they are contradictory. A radical empiricist is also a pragmatist, which means they do not think about truth in terms of correspondence with reality. Instead, a pragmatist thinks of truth as the belief that works the best when applied to life. And finally, a radical empiricist sees all elements of their actual experience as real, even if they do not fit in with their current understanding. They alter their understanding of reality to accommodate new experiences, rather than force new experiences to conform to their previous understanding of reality.

The late twentieth century philosopher Richard Rorty, perhaps following in the footsteps of William James, developed the notion of ironism. An ironist recognizes that everyone holds a bottom-line story about what they believe is real and true. This is what Rorty called their final vocabulary. It is the most foundational language they have for describing what is real and true. Most people assume that their final vocabulary, their story about what is ultimately real and true, is in fact a reflection of actual reality. Because of this, they will defend that final vocabulary with their last breath, if necessary, for beyond that they have nothing to stand on. They feel that if they give up their final vocabulary, they will be set adrift in a sea of confusion. They cannot let go of their bottom-line belief system. An ironist is someone who lives with continual doubt about their final vocabulary. They don't believe they have come to a final understanding of the truth, so they are always open and looking to grow their understanding. They also never believe that their final vocabulary is necessarily closer to reality than anyone else's. An ironist believes they can never ultimately know what reality is, and consequently can never be sure how near or far they are from it.

This is the problem of verisimilitude, which asks, "If we don't know what the objective truth is, then how can we tell which of two theories is more accurate? more real?" Karl Popper, the early twentieth century philosopher concluded that there *are* ways to know, yet others like James and Richard Rorty seem to think not. Or at least, in the case of Rorty, that it is better to not even try. This attitude is an extension, as I see it, of the existentialist position in philosophy. When I read existentialists like Søren Kierkegaard or Jean Paul Sartre, I hear them saying that we must choose what we believe and then give ourselves to it wholeheartedly. Kierkegaard coined the phrase "leap of faith" to signify just this. Our spiritual belief in God, he explained, cannot be proven like scientific facts. In fact, the power of believing in God comes from the fact that it demands faith. If we had proof, we wouldn't need faith. God without faith is powerless according to Kierkegaard. The willingness to believe with conviction and without proof, is where all the power comes from.

The trust that comes when we feel certain about reality is fragile. It cannot withstand challenges. When we believe that we are seeing the way reality is, then there is no room for other possibilities. There is no space for creativity. Our pursuit of higher dimensions of reality requires creativity. We need to be available to wildly alter our vision of reality based on each next experience. One of the things I want to share in this book is which inner attitude toward existence is most suitable for the demands of radical spiritual growth. The inner attitudes of an existentialist, an ironist, or a radical empiricist, point us in the right direction.

You might feel very confused by this last discussion and that is partly by design. I am not just trying to frustrate you, rather to open you up to possibility. You see, I don't want you to walk away from this book feeling like you know what is true. I don't want you to get stuck in any ideas of mine. I want you to feel confused about what is true and how you can ever know it, only to create more room inside you for discovery. The ideal is to be open to finding your own way through the maze of revelation. I want you to find your path, not follow mine. Open to your own experiences and come to your own conclusions and interpretations of them. There is no cookie cutter one-size-fits-all spiritual path. We are all unique, we all have unique circumstances and karmas. Our path must unfold as it is meant to, for us. Yes, there are parts of the journey that it seems we all need to travel, but in the end we all need to branch off and find our own way.

To me, this means that the way to evaluate the spiritual experiences we have and the interpretations we create to hold them is to think in terms of authenticity, rather than right and wrong. What interpretation feels most authentic and honest to us? What conclusions represent what we truly believe? At the start of the path, we adopt many ideas from books or teachers. There is a place for that and many of those ideas will become authentically our own. But as our path progresses it becomes more and more important that we listen to our own inner wisdom, knowing that the wisdom that flows through you is no different than that which flows through anyone else. You become capable of finding your own way as soon as you learn how to listen to the higher wisdom that is the source of your own awareness.

I have already told you about how I eventually came to the decision to leave the life of my marriage and career and join a spiritual community. That was an unprecedented leap in my life. I had never known anyone who had done such a thing. I didn't even know it was an option. It was a choice from a reality that was different to the one I had been a part of. For six months, I debated with myself about what to do. As I got to know people in the spiritual community, I learned, or at least came to believe, that the most serious seekers left everything for the path. As I contemplated this radical step in my life, I had a very existential realization.

I realized that every life I lived would either work out or not, and because I couldn't possibly know what a good life for me would look like, there was no way to improve the odds. Just like trying to guess which theory is closer to the truth when you don't know what the truth is, it is always going to be a 50/50 gamble. Since I could never know if the life I was living would work out in the end, I reasoned I should just do what felt most authentic to me. I could choose to join a spiritual community and it could turn out a mess. I could choose to live a conventional life, following all the rules, and still have it turn out a mess. I decided that since there was no way to know for sure I would choose what felt most true to me, and that was to join a spiritual community. And even if it turned out a mess, at least I had taken the chance to follow my dream, and for me, that counted.

I was a trained scientist so from that point on I decided to relate to this life as an experiment. Experiments never fail. Experiments just end. And when they end, whether they turn out the way you imagined they would or not, you learn from them. So, at the age of twenty-nine, I chose to devote myself to spiritual life full-time. That would be the experiment of my life and I would keep at it until the day I died. Only then would I see how it turned out. I would see what had resulted from my life as it ended, and I would take that wisdom with me into the next life if there was one. Many times, when I was challenged to the point of giving up, I would remember this attitude and realize that in order to let the experiment run its course, I had to stay on the path - I had to keep going to the end.

The experimental attitude toward life has served me well and another attitude that has served me has been to remain flexible and fluid as our spiritual life takes us through a succession of realizations and revelations. Each one of our breakthroughs opens a new realm of possibility to explore. William James used the image of a bird flying from perch to perch to describe how best to move through life. Each time we land on a moment of experience we respond to it as completely real, and yet we are always ready to fly on to something else when the wind blows. Another image I love is an underwater lava flow. From the ocean floor a red mass of molten rock squirts upward. It flows briefly then it hardens into a black rock. Eventually that rock begins to shake and when it breaks open another burst of red molten rock squirts forward. Through successive bursts of fluidity followed by hardening into solidity, we move like an underwater lava flow through life. We land, or harden, into a reality that is fixed and rigid at least for a time, but we are always ready to move to the next perch.

Our spiritual life progresses through the interpreted realities we create after each of our spiritual breakthroughs. We live in one understanding of reality and then we see a new and more powerful vision. We step wholeheartedly into that and live it, until we see more or deeper, and then we move on. I see spiritual life as an unending succession of discoveries. I believe that they are all heading toward something unimaginably magnificent, but what that might be, is far beyond my ability to even guess. I never want to get stuck in my next interpretation of reality. I always want to remain open to more. I would hate to think that what I have realized so far is all there is. I never want to come to the end of possibility. I always want there to be more to discover and explore. I believe that I am on a vast and unimaginable spiritual journey that has taken me through many lifetimes, into many worlds, in many dimensions of being. It boggles my mind to think about all the possibilities, but my spiritual experiences have convinced me beyond doubt, because I see myself as a free-floating center of awareness that flows into this world from another dimension. And in fact, that awareness flows into a new reality in each moment of experience. I am sure that my earthbound memory is not the limit of my existence. I am much more than that.

When I remembered my early childhood journeys to my cosmic self, I realized that I had come into this life from somewhere else. I wasn't born on my birthday. I had always been a cosmic being. I was a universal being coming into the limited form of a human being named Jeff, living on Earth for a short while. I felt strongly that this was not my first visit to Earth and that Earth was not the only planet I had visited. How did I know all this? I didn't, but it felt that way. It made sense to me. I remembered visiting my higher self as a young boy repeatedly. I knew exactly how to go back, and whenever I returned, I felt like I was home, back where I belonged, where I had come from. That was the feeling. I had forgotten about it completely for nearly forty years and I only remembered it when my meditation practice brought me back to the same place. Home again.

After that experience my whole life finally made complete sense. That crucial piece of missing information had made my life seem like an unfathomable mystery, but now everything was clear. I had come into this life remembering the magnificence of my cosmic being, and even more so, able to return to that state of being at will, so it is no wonder I was confused as a child. I never understood what anyone was doing here on Earth. I kept thinking that I would understand better when I was older, but the older I got, the more confusing it all was. People spent their time doing jobs they didn't like, waiting until they were old enough to stop. Nothing anyone talked about seemed very important. I asked a lot of questions, but the answers I received were unsatisfying.

I was a nervous child, prone to worry and anxiety. I developed eczema, I had few friends in school, and found navigating relationships difficult. I liked spending time on my own. I loved to draw. At school, I was always afraid of getting into trouble. I always worked hard to get good grades. My nervousness drove me crazy. When I was about seven, I spent time sitting in my father's car trying to make my mind stop. No matter how hard I tried, I couldn't do it. I couldn't make it stop. I tried slipping between thoughts, to emerge out of the other side of my mind. That didn't work either. I was stuck. Later, in high school, I would lay on the ground and look up at the stars or the clouds in the sky. I would feel how tiny I was in this big universe, and I would feel a tingle of energy in my spine. It was a small ecstasy that I would enjoy whenever I could. In college I smoked pot and dropped acid for a few years, but nothing helped my existential problem.

Now it all makes sense. By the time I was seven years old I had already forgotten my cosmic heritage. No wonder I found human life confusing. I was lost. I had lost my way back to my true self. Although I wasn't consciously aware of it, somewhere deep in my soul I knew this one life was much smaller than the actuality of who I was.

The huge mystery of my life was why I had left my first wife and joined a spiritual community. That radically unprecedented move had always been unfathomable to me, at least until I remembered my childhood experiences of cosmic awareness. Now it made perfect sense. The experience I had in that community unconsciously convinced me that this might be a way back home. Naturally, nothing else mattered. If you are born into human existence remembering universal being, nothing matters except finding a way back. Maybe that is why we generally don't remember. Imagine a planet full of people who all wanted to find a way out.

There is something I want to tell you. If you have been on a spiritual path, if you are reading this book, there is a reason. Oftentimes people will tell me that they have never had a spiritual experience. They act as if they are completely confused as to why they have ended up on a retreat or in a class with me. I never believe them. People don't end up on meditation retreats, or spend their time reading spiritual books, for no reason. If you have been on a spiritual path, or read books like this one, there is a very good reason. We don't embark on a spiritual path for money or because it's easy. And spiritual seekers are not the cool kids. We do this because we are compelled to, because we have no choice, and whether you remember or not, there is a reason.

There was a man who used to come to my retreats. His wife was a close student and he always used her as an excuse.

Sometimes I would ask people at the start why they had come. I wanted to know what they were hoping to find by being there. He would always say something like, "She made me come" pointing to his wife. Over time I learned that he also did at least one ten-day Buddhist meditation retreat each year because his wife made him. And he had done other spiritual work for decades. Sometimes I would challenge him saying that he must be here for a reason beyond just that his wife made him. He would laugh it off and tell me his wife was very persuasive. He would tell me he never had a spiritual experience in his life. I didn't believe him.

During one of the retreats he attended, I had everyone do a dialog exercise. I asked them to share in detail about the most powerful spiritual experience they remember. The instructions were specific, and included describing in detail what they had experienced, and they were asked to not just talk about it, but to allow themselves to feel it again in the present. I asked people to allow the memory of that experience to enter their body as they spoke and describe what they were experiencing directly. I didn't want them to just share a memory of a past event. I wanted them to reignite the experience in their hearts and minds and let it speak through them. I have done this exercise many times on retreats and it is always powerful.

After the exercise I asked if some people would be willing to share and I was pleasantly surprised to see that the man whose wife had forced him to come had his hand up. I could see he was smiling, and he looked radiant. I asked him to share, and he began to speak excitedly. He told me that he had just had an amazing experience. He remembered a spiritual breakthrough he had when he was in his twenties. During the exercise he went back to describe some dim memory of something that had happened. As he was sharing about the experience it opened inside him. Suddenly he remembered it all vividly. He described a dramatic experience of oneness and his inability to integrate it into his life. It was the most magnificent thing he had ever experienced, and it made him question everything about life. He could not believe he had forgotten about something so significant.

Now it all made sense to him, and to me. That is why he had done so many personal transformation courses throughout his life. It made sense that he did long Buddhist meditation retreats every year. He was not coming to my retreats just because his wife made him. He was coming because somewhere inside he remembered what he had experienced, and he wanted to rediscover it.

You may be one of those people who doesn't think they know why they spend so much of their energy on a spiritual path. You may be convinced that you haven't had any spiritual experiences. If you are on a spiritual path, and you read books like this, it cannot be true. Just because you don't remember your reasons, doesn't mean you don't have any. The spiritual path that we embark on in human form is a small part of an unimaginably vast journey. It is not ours alone. It is the journey of a universal being that wants to find itself in human form. That cosmic self has become manifest here on earth as you, and me, and everyone else. The awareness and compassion that radiates through our mind and personality comes from that universal being. We are that. We don't become the cosmic self when we remember who we really are. We are the cosmic self whether we remember or not. Our remembering or forgetting doesn't change the fact. We are a universal being, a cosmic self, and our experiences of universal awareness reveal that to us.

You can see how the trail of breadcrumbs that our spiritual experiences leave behind can get pretty wild. That is why, if we want to follow them, we need to adopt an inner attitude that is fluid and free. We need to embrace every experience we have as real, without getting attached to it. What does it mean to embrace an experience as real? It means being willing to act on it. It means being willing to make decisions and take actions as if it were real, even though we know that the truth of it might be called into question and replaced by a higher truth at any moment. We stake our lives on the reality of this moment, always ready to pivot with the next revelation. We commit to what is, while remaining open to the ever-expanding new possibilities that will inevitably emerge. We act with conviction at every moment, but we don't get stuck. We are not afraid to be wrong about what we think is real, because we know we will always be. There is no end to truth and there is no end to mystery.

CHAPTER SEVEN

Higher Purpose

"Many poets are not poets for the same reason that many religious men are not saints: they never succeed in being themselves. They never get around to being the particular poet or the particular monk they are intended to be by God. They never become the man or the artist who is called for by all the circumstances of their individual lives."

~ Thomas Merton

I HAVE TWO MORE EXPERIENCES to share before this exploration is over. The first happened about three years after the retreat where I experienced kundalini awakening, cosmic awareness, and constant consciousness. In fact, I think that this next experience was the culmination of an opening that started on that retreat three years earlier. I have seen this in myself and others many times. We have an experience of breakthrough and then there is a period in which that breakthrough is being integrated. Then there is a completion experience which activates the potentials that were inherent in the initial opening.

For the moment, let's use different names for these two kinds of spiritual experiences. We will call one a spiritual opening and the other a spiritual activation. In actuality I think it is more accurate to say that every spiritual experience plays both of these roles because they are the fulfillment of everything that came before, and at the very same time they awaken us to more.

The retreat on which I experienced such wondrous openings was the completion and fulfillment of years of dedicated spiritual work and a lifetime of spiritual searching. During that retreat, which has become the defining event in my earthly existence, I experienced dozens of powerful openings, only a few of which I have explored in detail in this book. Those openings were the fulfillment of the initial opening I had when I first left the world that I knew to join a spiritual community and pursue the miraculous. The possibility that opened for me the day I experienced the true risk of life was the chance to live a life dedicated entirely to spiritual pursuits. I remember very distinctly the feeling of amazement that this was possible. I had been told since early childhood that I would grow up, find a career, get married and have children. I had some choice around which career I pursued, and whom I would marry, but I wasn't aware of any other options.

When I met my spiritual teacher and his community, I saw something else, something that I had never imagined. I could live a spiritual life outside of the context of being a catholic monk, which was in fact an option I had contemplated. This was different. I could pursue spiritual knowledge and experience and, I could find inner awakening and transformation. It was possible to transform and the means to do it existed. This was the revelation that compelled me to step out of the conventional life that I was living and join, what by many accounts could be called a cult. I'm not afraid of the word cult because to me it just means an enclosed social system that demands that its members conform to a particular worldview. By that definition we all live in several cults throughout our lifetimes. The engineering firm I worked in was just as much a cult as my spiritual community. We all live in cults, the more important question to ask is, are they good for us? And are they good for the world?

The possibility that compelled me to leave my life and leap into a situation that probably should have terrified me was the notion that I could live a life dedicated to awakening and find what I was looking for. For the next eight years I worked hard to become an upstanding, prominent, and well-loved member of the community. I managed to become just that, and along the way I had many spiritual experiences. Each next experience inspired me forward and fueled my passion for more. But it wasn't until I found myself on retreat eight years later that the culmination of that promise came to full fruition. During those two months I experienced openings every day that revealed more and more dramatically the truth of who I was. As I have already discussed, I discovered that my life energy comes directly from the creative source of the cosmos, that I came into this life with a living connection to my universal nature, and that the source of my awareness is the consciousness of the universe. I had discovered my truest self. The vision that had compelled me to live a spiritual life had come to a profound degree of fulfillment.

At the same time, these realizations opened new mysteries. The possibility that grabs me now was the possibility of creating a human life that was a clear reflection of everything that I had realized. For the next three years in fits and starts those of us who had been on retreat together, as well as others in the community, struggled to discern how to live the revelations we had been blessed with. I have already mentioned that some of us started leading discussion groups to ignite collective awakening. Those groups went very well for a time. Many people attended them all over the world and we trained more and more people to facilitate them. However, eventually it became unsatisfying. People were coming, but they seemed mainly interested in having repeated experiences of the intimacy and connection of collective awakening. The implications beyond the experience didn't seem to be of much interest to many people. Our meetings started to feel like spiritual entertainment and gradually we stopped doing them.

After that retreat many of us felt compelled to realize the full potential of what we had experienced. We wanted to discover and manifest the potential of those experiences for life. We wanted to know what the purpose of those experiences was. The initial eight years I spent in a spiritual community were all about having experiences of realization, but once that realization had been attained, I was looking for a purpose to fulfill, and it seemed that just duplicating that experience wasn't it. The attention of the community turned inward once again as we searched for the meaning of what we had discovered. We started talking about going beyond periodically experiencing the miracle of collective awakening, which we often did, into a stabilized state of that miracle as a community. We wanted to give birth to what we called a 'higher we,' so that it could remain permanently alive between us.

After a few years it began to happen. Our community was spread throughout the world and over the course of about a month, people everywhere seemed to be having similar experiences of a new depth of the higher we. It was thrilling. For me this time became the fulfillment of the opening that had happened on retreat. It catapulted me into a new life with a new purpose. The moment of transition came while I was on yet another retreat in India with my teacher. I had accompanied him on a teaching trip as a participant and as his assistant. And during this retreat, which I see as the fruition of the earlier long retreat, my life radically shifted again.

I remember being in the room with about one hundred people in attendance at the retreat. They were mostly Indian people. My teacher was sitting in the front, and he was speaking eloquently about the fact that our consciousness is coming from the universe itself. We are the universe speaking. As he spoke, I found myself listening intently and looking around the room. I saw that all the faces were transfixed in rapped attention, eyes wide open looking at the animated speaker. My teacher was speaking excitedly, arms moving and gesturing as he explained himself. I kept looking back and forth between the people in the audience watching the teacher speaking. The energetic dynamic in the room became more and more obvious.

Suddenly everything looked different. My teacher wasn't speaking words that he was making up. He was opening his mouth and words were coming through from a source beyond. Words were not being propelled into the room by the teacher, they were being pulled out of him by the attention in the room. The people in the room were literally pulling the teachings into the room with their enthusiastic attention. This teaching would not happen without an audience to pull it forth. My teacher was not the originator of the teaching, he was the vehicle, the transmitter, for words and ideas that were coming from beyond him.

As I watched I became more and more mesmerized by what was unfolding in front of me. I saw that the higher mind of the universal being was pulling itself into existence. The attention of the audience was acting as a magnet, pulling itself forward. My teacher was acting as the mouthpiece. I saw that the true greatness of a teacher is not the wisdom they hold inside, but their willingness to be open and receptive so that wisdom from beyond them can pour through. What I was watching felt sacred and holy. It was an exchange of the cosmos to itself.

Everyone present was taking part in a birthing process. Everyone was essential to the final execution. For many years I worked with this teacher. I acted as his personal assistant, by his side day and night for a good deal of those years. I saw both his brilliance and his deficiencies at different times, but it was on this occasion that I saw the true greatness of being a teacher. In his willingness to surrender to his own passion for higher truth he allowed himself to be empty and free enough so that words from beyond could pass through. I was awed by the sacred function being played. As the teaching went on, I stopped seeing an audience and a teacher. I saw only an energetic exchange. I saw how some higher being was pouring the energy of wisdom and love into this world. I saw energy emerging with the words that were spoken and entering the eyes and ears of those in the room. The universe was feeding itself.

When the teaching was over, I did not walk out by my teacher's side as I usually would. Instead, I walked twenty paces behind. I was awed by the vision I had seen and unable to speak. My teacher, seeing my odd behavior, just thought I was acting weird. When we arrived at his apartment, he asked me what was the matter. I remember sitting on the floor at his feet and explaining as best I could what I had seen. As I spoke his demeanor changed. He was no longer angry. He went from curious, to interested, to delighted. He acknowledged that I had seen something very important, and he told me to think about what I had seen.

I knew from that day forward that my destiny was to serve this function. I saw how it was possible to serve the world by allowing a wisdom greater than my own to speak through me, and to allow a love, bigger than my heart could possibly hold, to care through me. This is what I knew I had to do. Three years earlier on retreat I had opened to the universal being that is our true source. Now I was being called to serve that being as a mouthpiece and an ambassador. I knew that I was not a perfect vehicle for this function, but I also knew that I could grow and open and develop.

A few months later I held my first public daylong retreat in New York City. The success of that event led to the formation of a group of about forty people who were committed to meeting once a week by conference call. The conference calls became a weekly webcast that would attract hundreds of listeners over the next two years. Soon I was teaching throughout the United States, Canada, Europe, and Australia. It has been fifteen years since my public teaching career began. What I have taught, and to whom, has shifted at different times over the years, but I have never stopped teaching. And whenever I teach, I do my best to stay true to the vision I had on that retreat. I do my best to be empty and available for the wisdom that wants to come through. And I always try to remember that the wisdom is not mine. It is a gift from the same source that gives me life.

When I teach, if I have ideas about what I want to say, I like to share them as quickly as possible so that I have nothing left to say because I want to stand in front of my audience with nothing so that surrender to higher wisdom is the only option left. I always have a little fear that nothing will come, but so far, it always has. When leading retreats I have learned not to plan too much in advance because once the retreat starts it has a life of its own. Very little, if anything, I think of beforehand will ever be repeated on retreat. I find when I teach that the people there in front of me pull the words out, just like I saw happen that day in India. Often people tell me that I am very good at public speaking, but what I am good at is allowing something to speak through me. Receiving this higher calling was the fruition of the retreat I had been on three years earlier. What opened on that retreat had come in search of another spokesperson in the world.

As I began to teach, it didn't feel like a choice. The desire to share all that I had experienced was so strong I felt powerless to stop it. I also know that I have worked tirelessly for nearly two decades to create platforms and structures that allow me to continue doing what I love. Destiny might be choiceless, but it is not inevitable. It is a kind of participatory choiceless-ness. We are pushed into it, but we must also pick up the ball and run. Spirit can do anything, but only with our cooperation. I believe that you have found this book so that you can discover and embrace your own higher destiny. I wrote this book so that you could discover something about yourself. I wanted you to see yourself in my story, to hear your own wisdom in my words, to find your destiny along with the courage and willingness to manifest it.

The cosmos is an awakening being that we are all a part of. The consciousness of this universe is waking up though all the conscious beings in it. Our consciousness belongs to the cosmos. We are that. The Hindu teachings that I have studied come alive in this vision. Brahman is the universal being. Atman is the in-dividual expression of that universal being. Awakening means realizing that our Atman is not separate from, but one with, Brahman. We are that.

In the vision of a living cosmos awakening to its true nature, I have discovered a vision that fits my spiritual experience and makes radical sense to me. I have had this vision confirmed so often in so many ways that I cannot deny it. The universal being is our source, and it wants greater access to the manifest world that we live in. Our spiritual journey was never about us. It was always about opening wider so that a universal source could enter the world through us. It was never our awakening. It was always about the awakening of the cosmos. The cosmos has been lost in a dream that says it is only human when it is much more than that. The cosmos is waking up to its true existence. At the same time, I, and all of us, are not separate from that awakening cosmos. We have forgotten our true selves as a universal being. We have been lost in the idea of being only a person on Earth when we are much more than that. From a universal point of view, a cosmic being is waking up to itself. From the individual human point of view, we are waking up to our true self as a cosmic being.

In the grand process of universal awakening, many of us are called to play a role. Some of us are called to teach in the way that I have been. Others are called to paint, or dance or be exceptional in any number of pursuits. When we find and express our true passions and gifts, we become an expression of the higher being in the world. The path laid out by our spiritual experiences reveals our purpose and then it is up to us to shine. When we shine with our true inner light, we become what I call an Artist of Possibility. Each in our own way, illuminates new possibilities and potentials. In my journey, the energy that had been focused on seeking, found what it was looking for, and then was ready to be shared.

The last experience I want to share has to do with the end of the spiritual path. We work hard on our spiritual journey.

We practice, study, attend retreats and take programs. We learn and we grow and believe that in the end it will all lead to something. We have ideas and visions of what our final experience of letting go will be like. We imagine that we will be swept up and catapulted into a state of consciousness which will answer every prayer we have ever had. Our spiritual dream will come true, and we will be done with the path.

When this next experience happened, it had been twenty years since I joined a spiritual community. It had been twelve years since the long retreat when I opened to the energy of kundalini, cosmic awareness, and the source of constant consciousness. It had been seven years since I had begun teaching all over the world. And I was on yet another long retreat. I probably couldn't count how many long retreats I have done, but I know that each time I started one it was with the energy of a racehorse waiting to run. I was always determined to give more than I ever had before. And even after so many years, this retreat was no exception. I sat on my cushion ready to start the first hour of practice with complete gusto. The bell rang, and I had an immediate realization. I didn't have the energy to do this again, I just couldn't. Initially I was terrified. I thought I had lost my spiritual passion and drive. I felt like I was giving up on myself and the possibility of realizing my full potential. I had feared this moment might come. I had worried that I would someday just run out of energy for the spiritual path, that I would lose my will and give up. And now it had happened. What would I do now?

A moment later everything changed. I realized that I had not lost my spiritual drive. I just didn't need any more spiritual experiences. For nearly twenty years I had given all my energy and attention to my spiritual life. I had had more breakthrough experiences than I could possibly remember. For years I had done my spiritual practice with all my heart and soul because I was convinced that I would eventually have a realization that would finish my quest. What I was seeing now was that there was no experience I could possibly have at this point that would make me anymore convinced, or any more certain about who I really was as a cosmic being. I didn't have energy to give to the retreat because I no longer needed any more proof. I was done.

The spiritual path does not necessarily come to an end in a final glorious moment of ultimate revelation. Sometimes, perhaps more often than not, it comes to an end with a simple recognition that we are done. We know who we are, and we understand what matters. Our hearts and minds are open, and we don't need any more spiritual experiences to convince us. The end of spiritual seeking is much less about finding than it is about being done seeking. Finding has more to do with ending the search than it does with discovery. As I sat there on my cushion, I realized that everything was fine. Here on Earth, I was a human being that was born on my birthday living my life. Before this life I was a cosmic being. I was the consciousness of the universe. The consciousness that was experiencing itself as Jeff sitting on a cushion at the start of a retreat was that same universal consciousness. The awareness that was realizing that Jeff didn't need any more proof of who he was, was the same universal being realizing itself through me. I had always been a universal being even before Jeff was aware of it. Jeff didn't become a universal being when he realized it. He always was that. I had no doubt.

I sat on my cushion having been quietly stunned into submission. I had ten days of silent retreat ahead of me and I didn't need anything. What was I going to do? Nothing. I didn't need to do anything. I just sat there on my cushion. I saw the movement of thought and feeling in my mind. I didn't need to do anything about any of it. None of it mattered. It was just a mind thinking and feeling. None of it had anything to do with me. I didn't need my mind to be quiet. I didn't need to have any experience of revelation. I was fine. So, I just sat there. I was completely relaxed. There was absolutely no tension because I had no aspiration. I was free.

That hour of meditation was, in a way, the very first true hour of meditation I had done in all my twenty years of devoted practice. I realized that true meditation can only happen after we are done seeking. It's been almost another decade since I realized that I had no need for more proof, and I have never gone back to feeling the need for any. That doesn't mean that those were easy years. In fact, they included some of the most challenging times of my life because it was in that period that the spiritual community I lived in, disbanded in an undeniably inelegant way. It also doesn't mean that I stopped growing. I was exactly who I was with all the same strengths and weaknesses. I still needed to grow in all the same ways. The only thing that changed was that existentially I was fine. I didn't need anything to be fundamentally ok. Now that I knew who I was as a cosmic being, I was finally content with being Jeff in his human life. Jeff was growing and becoming increasingly capable of expressing the cosmic source. Jeff was far from perfect, but he would continue to grow.

What became obvious to me, was that our spiritual growth happens more despite our efforts, than because of them. Yes, we practice, study, and work, but the whole time we don't really know what we are working toward. The point of existential release cannot be imagined. If it happens, it just happens. It is always a matter of grace, a gift from the divine. Spiritual growth is not an activity that we do, in the same way that physical growth is not something we do. You can't hang by your arms to grow taller. Growth can't be forced; it can only be allowed. In the right atmosphere, with the right nutrients, growth happens. Spiritual growth is the same. In the right atmosphere, with the right nutrients, spiritual growth happens. This planet and the circumstances of your own life provide that atmosphere. The triumphs and obstacles that you experience in life provide the nutrients you need for growth. Growth happens best when we let it happen without trying to help it along. Imagine a small child trying to help you with something more complicated than they are capable of. They can't help at all no matter how sincerely they want to. We are like this when it comes to our spiritual growth.

As spiritual aspirants the one thing we can do is learn how to let go. We must stop seeking and learn to be whole and complete right now. Then, once we have let go, the process of spiritual growth will continue to move freely through us. Our job is to surrender; the rest is up to the divine. Imagine you are driving a car that is completely capable of driving itself. The car can not only drive on autopilot, but it has also downloaded the perfect route to your destination. All you need to do is let go of the steering wheel and it will get you there, but you won't let go. Even though you don't know the route you keep trying to steer the car yourself. You can't help this way. You can only help by letting go. Once you let go the car will drive itself. When I teach, I am always ultimately teaching people to let go and allow the process of growth to take them.

That day on the cushion at the start of yet another retreat, Jeff's spiritual search came to an end. From one point of view, he had been fighting a war of attrition without realizing it. For years he had given so much of himself and endured so much hardship until he just couldn't do it anymore. He lost the war because he simply couldn't continue the fight. From another point of view, he had just been a very stubborn seeker. Many of the experiences he had over those many years of seeking could have been enough to end the search. Any one of them potentially provided all the proof Jeff needed to let go, but he had been stubbornly holding out for more. In the end he had no more energy to continue, and he simultaneously realized that he already had everything he needed.

The spiritual path comes to an end when we give up the search. What any of us need to be able to do that, we cannot know. We all have a different karma. For some it might be one spiritual insight, for me it was twenty years' worth. The spiritual path of the individual is the path that takes us to the place where we are finally ready to stop seeking. Where we are finally content with who we are. That path will look different for everyone. I don't think we can avoid the path we must take. If your path is going to involve hardship and pain, then that is what it will contain. If your path is centered on joy and wellbeing, then that is what it will be. If you are destined to search for decades, then you will. If your destiny is to be illuminated in a random moment with no conscious spiritual path leading up to it, then you can be sure that is what will happen.

What I want to tell you now, is that whatever your path is, the end result will invariably be that you give up searching. You will realize that you could have let go at any time. There was no need to go through all the trials and tribulations before letting go. And if you feel that you haven't let go yet, I want to tell you that you can right now. Nothing more needs to happen. You can let go and give up, and the path of your continued growth will unfold all the better for it. Of course, if it is your destiny to keep seeking for twenty more years, there is no way for you to avoid it. Nothing I tell you here will convince you to let go unless it is your time to do so. So, you might ask, why write all this if none of it can help? The answer is because it might be your time and these words might be exactly what you need to hear to trigger your final release. I offer them just in case it is.

If it is not your time, then everything that I have shared in this book is offered as food for thought. The examples of my own experiences and the ways I have interpreted them and drawn conclusions about life from them, might help you navigate your own path wherever it leads you. Some of us find it impossible to just live in the world as we found it. We won't go quietly along being the person everyone tells us that we are. We know, somewhere deep inside that we are more than that. We have, in a peak experience, or some now forgotten moment, glimpsed our true nature and we can't be satisfied with less.

If this describes you then I have some advice. Pay careful attention to your spiritual experiences. Think about what they are telling you about reality and how it works. Be open to even the wildest possibilities. Once you have found an understanding of your experience that resonates deeply in your heart, hold on to it with all your might. Make choices that reflect what you now know about reality. Allow your life to be shaped by your deepest realization. And most importantly continue to be open. Never conclude that you know all there is to know. Never assume that you cannot be wrong about what you think. Keep paying attention to your realizations and revelations and jump in with both feet as soon as you realize that reality is different than you thought. This is how I have lived my life. I have often been wrong, and I have made many mistakes, but looking back on it now, I don't regret any of it. The experiment continues.

Surround yourself with the most spiritually nutritious and energetically alive circumstances you can find. Seek out and befriend like-minded souls. Pursue your spiritual passion with your whole heart. Allow yourself to be blessed by whatever gifts divinity offers. Take those gifts seriously and let your life be guided by them. Don't be overly concerned with where the path is taking you. Don't worry about where you might be in the middle of it all. Live your spiritual experiences fully and know that you were born of a cosmic being and you are still that.

About the Author

Jeff Carreira is a meditation teacher, mystical philosopher and author who works with a growing number of people throughout the world. As a teacher, he offers retreats and courses guiding individuals in a form of meditation he refers to as *The Art of Conscious Contentment*. Through this simple and effective technique, he has led thousands of people in a journey beyond the confines of fear and self-concern into the expansive liberated awareness that is our true home.

As a philosopher, Jeff is interested in defining a new way of being in the world that will move us from our current paradigm of separation and isolation into an emerging paradigm of unity and wholeness. In his books and lectures, he explores revolutionary ideas in the domains of spirituality, consciousness, and human development. He creates courses and programs that encourage people to question their most foundational experience of reality until previously held assumptions fall away leaving space for a dramatically new understanding to emerge.

Jeff is passionate about the potential ideas have to shape how we perceive reality and how we live together. His enthusiasm for learning is infectious, and he has taught at colleges and universities throughout the world.

> *In a world in which university education is often thought of as a vocational certificate, seeing someone obviously relishing the acquisition and sharing of knowledge for its own sake is inspiring.*

— Dr. William O. Shropshire, Provost and Professor Emeritus Ogelthorpe University

Jeff is the author of numerous books including *American Awakening, Philosophy Is Not a Luxury, The Soul of a New Self, Paradigm Shifting*, and *The Art of Conscious Contentment*.

For more information visit: jeffcarreira.com

Made in United States
Troutdale, OR
06/19/2023

10664003R10096